RESURRECTION OF VALUES

John Walchars, S.J.

RESURRECTION OF VALUES

CROSSROAD · NEW YORK

1986
The Crossroad Publishing Company
370 Lexington Avenue, New York, N.Y. 10017

Printed in the United States of America

Library of Congress Cataloging-in-Publication Data

Walchars, John.
  Resurrection of values.

    1. Christian life—Catholic authors. 2. Values.
I. Title.
BX2350.2.W298   1986   248.4'82   86-6403
ISBN 0-8245-0746-0

To
My Jesuit Community
At Weston

Acknowledgment to
CAROLINA ACCORSI
and
VIRGINIA MALACHOWSKI
with appreciation
for their help and encouragement

Epigram verses and manuscript preparation
by Virginia Malachowski

Contents

Preface

We the people of our times have not lost our way as some less-articulated prophets predicate; we the people of our times are only searching for better ways to cope with a challenging and thought-provoking future. In a civilization where long-cherished values have departed and new ones are slow to arrive, historical opportunities arise that are receptive to very exciting concepts. Periods of transition interest our minds far more intensely than centuries of security and peace. Those who are open to change will exercise a greater impact on the shape of our tomorrows. The more daring usually prevail.

A predominant characteristic of present thinking is its preference for thoughts in development. Forces that call for new thinking are preferred to ideas that are stagnant. The unchangeable elements, even when proven correct by centuries of use, mean less to our present generation than perspectives with more recent meaning. The creative spark of a new and presumedly better world fascinates the imagination of the growing generation.

The book of God, our Bible, is still the best seller on the market of the world. People in all walks of life hunger for the wisdom contained in the Holy Book. Its message, however, is expected to be lived, not simply interpreted. The word of God reincarnated in our concerns for the poor and forgotten is still the ultimate authority that illuminates our minds. God is not expected to change; the way we live His message has to be changed!

Most of us like to be classified as progressive. Such an identification, however, is considered for the better only if it is linked to respect and love for tradition. As long as these modern minds preserve a clear and marked continuity with the past, without the senseless compromises of the present, they offer a valuable contribution toward building a hopeful future. To be receptive to our changing world with all of its fascinating progress and still retain a clearly defined, time-honored Christian position reflects maturity of great value. No one can contribute everlasting values without drawing sustenance from the *source* of everlasting values . . . the Church. The ethical man or woman is not enough; the Christian is needed if the tide is to be turned.

The Church of today is not expected to bow in servility to the spirit of our times. Such a submission would be fatal to the revelations of Christ. It is up to our priests, ministers and Sisters to take the achievements of our present civilization seriously and to study prevailing thought diligently with the one burning desire to redeem our century.

The purpose of the following chapters is to direct the inquisitive mind toward perspectives of contemporary ideas that are in harmony with eternal destiny. Aware that many publications easily accommodate the questionable ideals in vogue, I found it necessary to stress important moral values and ethical convictions that in my opinion invigorate Christian thinking.

Chapter 1

CHARISMA

Charisma is a gift
Of inborn, hidden treasure;
A talent to be shared
And lived to fullest measure.

Whenever the word *charisma* is mentioned, we immediately connect the magical expression with the lives of artistic personalities, diplomatic figures or other popular heroes. People glorified on our entertainment screens or in our daily headlines are usually considered to be endowed with the luxuries of this special gift. How else could they have climbed to the top of the ladder if they did not possess the extraordinary faculties that distinguish them from the ordinary man or woman? The person who commands our attention by way of looks, voice or attractive talents is held in awe and admiration.

Obviously some of our outstanding performers do have superior abilities that encourage them to strive for the top positions in their chosen fields. Yet it would be a serious error to conclude that the rest of us were neglected by the watchful eye of our Creator. The moment we presume that charisma belongs to the famous alone, we lose sight of the fact that God gave every human being a special sign of uniqueness. Even though our names never parade in public, we also have been singled out by God to function in the grandiose orchestration of redemption. Each one of us has been given particular gifts that we are expected to use in the search for fulfillment.

How many of us are aware of our own charisma? Can we identify the nature of this personal gift from God? Do we make a distinctive effort to integrate it into the mainstream of our lives? If we succeed in the realization of our charisma, it will gradually become a prominent factor in the development of our personality. If we fail, however, we forfeit an unmistakable source of strength and inspiration.

Charisma, often mysterious and elusive, can be recognized as an inner intelligence that gives us a deeper understanding of the ultimate reasons of life. Rare insight and deep comprehension of problems arise from the capacities that are inborn rather than acquired. Certainly, education can inspire the birth of thoughts, but innate illumination provides a more incisive light in the complexities of issues. This inner perception allows us to verbalize and act with clarity and precision even in times of distractions and confusion. The gift of knowledge called charisma enables us to establish norms and directions for our never-ending search of truth.

A sign of this talent is its ability to favor lasting values over transitory sophistication. In fidelity to its supernatural origin, it perceives life on earth not as an end in itself but as a preface to the future experience with our Redeemer. Since our natural impulses tend to draw our attention to material fascinations, we need this intelligence to act as a corrective, a reminder that the narrow path is the only avenue into the eternal kingdom. Our charisma, making itself heard as the voice of conscience, orients our mind toward the ideals that favor destiny. To understand goodness is to possess it; to embrace evil is to promote it. Those not tuned into faith are easily led to accept majority opinions as final. "As long as everyone is doing it, it must be all right!" When we allow charisma to influence the mental and emotional stability of our personality, it can also be a stabilizer of aroused sensitivities.

Feelings that advocate mercy, understanding and love help us to recognize God's endowment to us. When there is a consistent pull of sympathy in one direction, we can assume our charisma is fully alive and geared for action. Not that this mysterious gift is imperturbable in its drive; impulsive outbursts are totally compatible with its service. Various responses and diversity in temperament may obscure the real trend of the personality, but seldom do they obliterate the true charisma.

Boredom, an unavoidable element of life, is not beyond the redemptive powers of charisma. Whereas most of us suffer from the weight of tedious repetitions, this invisible force revives the energies needed to cope with the sameness of life. If an ordinary day is to be seen equally as attractive as the day of excitement, the miracle of this divine skill is needed to remind us of all the things awaiting our interest. A mind challenged by opportunities seldom tires of itself. With our determination and stamina renewed, we quickly numb the attacks of boredom.

The gift of charisma does not include a guarantee of success. Adjustments are necessary between the role it plays and the exigencies of life. If we yield generously to the inspirations of our "heavenly monitor," disagreements rarely flare into conflicts. The forgiving word, the sympathetic gesture, the loving touch melt the ice of suspicions and doubt. As an arbiter and guide, this superior mastery not only focuses on an immediate problem, it also influences the final outcome with penetrating clarity. Rewarding experiences come into existence when a favorable response is made to the nudgings "from above." Ignoring or refusing the suggestions of "our better self" can easily result in a regretful and devastating encounter.

It lies within the nature of a gift that it be shared. What we have received has to be given; those we love have a right to profit from our uniqueness. Even people we are not overly fond of are entitled to glean from our blessings. Friends who have not yet discovered what we have already found should be granted access to our insight and understanding. Human relationships depend on the quality of all parties involved. The more superior the advance of one, the more lasting the benefits for the other. After all, isn't the concern for others a major part of responsibility?

An important advantage of charisma is that it offers continuing support in our search for identity. We can rely on many a guiding pointer of this inner counselor for ideas that will make us aware of what we are and what we are not. The complexities of our personality are so intertwined with the powers which generate charisma that the growth periods of both are strongly united. For example, if our particular imprint is patience, the accent of growth will lie on tolerance and endurance; if our gift is forgiveness, a sympathetic and graceful personality will develop. The elements that condition the unfolding of the self also affects the evolution of the skills.

God the giver expects us to be the performer. When we are blessed with extraordinary charisma, our actions have to reflect it in a depth of thought and maturity of judgment. People will accept guidance when it is offered without superficiality. On the other hand, the advice that lacks solid foundation and is based on impetuous suppositions is usually resented. Performance alone does not establish the ultimate criterion; it has to be supported by sincere and unselfish motivations. No matter how impressive the deed, it cannot produce lasting satisfaction without inner inspiration.

People are their own worst enemy! Men and women in every walk of life carry an inner treasure without capitalizing on its presence. Timidity in character and the fear of failing curtail their enthusiasm for any creative response. Even when the value of a charisma is known, its consequences are not always accepted because of pride. Close human relationships that develop their own patterns of survival prefer to remain independent of a higher inspiration; the need to develop and multiply talents is not recognized. Sometimes, family tensions burst out of control because members are not granted enough space for individual uniqueness to grow. Can the charisma of peace really bring peace if only one hand is reaching out?

Divine riches express themselves in diversity. The unique

abilities God has given to one person are unlike the abilities given to another. It was St. Paul who realized, perhaps better than any other apostle, that the divine gifts were of tremendous variety. In his first letter to the Corinthians, he speaks of the different instincts that can trace their origin to heaven: faith, wisdom, preaching, healing, prophesy, tongues and the performance of miracles. This letter by no means exhausts the possibilities in which a charisma would incarnate itself: others would include trust, hope, forgiveness and compassion. Our Divine Master has given us a freedom of emotions, and yet we expect others to conform to our ways. More than once have hostile reactions forced the spontaneous expressions of charisma to a harmful standstill. Why is it so difficult for someone to allow another person the right to live a special destiny? If our Lord offers us diversity, why should we look for sameness? Are we being fair when we expect our loved ones to adjust to our concepts of perfection?

Holy Scripture and human experience both confirm the thought that *love* is the most enlightening charisma. For the sake of love, Christ became human; in the name of love, a human being becomes Christlike. Many a stunning presentation is inspired by the enthusiasm and dedication stimulated by a "heart on fire." Artists everywhere freely acknowledge that some of their works were completed as immortal masterpieces because love put wings on their performances. Devotion and affection not only enrich our mental capacities, they also induce us to offer our physical energies for the good of the beloved. Very often, someone will forgo a personal interest to allow time for the interest of the friend to be developed. And although not a common occurrence, unusual circumstances of life can generate so much love that one person will sacrifice the self so that another person can survive.

To love abundantly is to live abundantly; to love forever is to live forever. Life in its essence is nothing more or less than love made visible. Only the actions that exteriorize the qualities of our heartfelt devotion will be accepted in our favor at the divine judgment. The things we do to cater to self and feed the ego will be considered "in vain" by God himself. Deeds fulfilled in the name of love or for the sake of God, identical ideals in the final analysis, are the only ones worthy of divine recognition.

In the drama of charisma, triumphs and defeats are close neighbors. Among the many sufferings sustained by human beings, the betrayal of a personal charisma is a most pitiful and degrading experience. When the inner voice of God, always present in a charisma, is silenced by the voice of man, a conflict arises that has to be settled in the conscience of each individual. For the sake of political advantages or vocational promotion, leaders whose direction is based on short-lived pleasures and financial rewards will expect us to give up the timeless values of hope, love and honor. Those of us who are not strong enough to resist will yield to the pressures of promise and security. Such exchanges may look attractive for the *now* but will become distasteful in the *later*.

Even with charisma, the chosen path will not always lead us to the road of achievement; occasionally, the way will peter out into a trackless course of disappointment. At such a time, however, by accepting charisma as our guide, we can gaze upward with the hope of discovering among the millions of celestial bodies the one "star" radiating a light especially for us. This one star, however modest or insignificant, will outshine all others because we believe it can lead us back to a safe and loving shelter. In a world full of people, it speaks to us alone; only we are able to fathom the particular meaning and destiny of our heavenly sign. It is a time to sing and dance because in this "star of stars" we have found our heavenly charisma.

Chapter 2

SLOWING DOWN

Oh Lord I need to slow me down,
My time is running fast;
Unless I change this hurried pace
I'll only know my past!

Few characteristics reflect contemporary mores and manners better than the ominous terms of haste and turmoil. When people venture over the thresholds of their serene homes into the noisy turbulence of the highways, they realize that in order to match the speed of modern excitement, the only direction to follow is *push, hurry, run.* Some of them feel that by standing still or slowing down, their chances for success are jeopardized. The need to rush becomes such a driving obsession that even when they hurry, there is the strange sensation of already being late! It seems that everyone around, in front or behind, sets a pace that needs to be surpassed. The race is joined with only one purpose in mind . . . to win. Whether the price paid for staying in contention is worth its reward rarely changes their decision. Although physical strains and emotional anxieties may affect their sanity, seldom do these hazards of modern living slow people down; they know that when energies are exhausted, chemical stimulants are available to give back the illusion of power and strength.

Time is the one commodity to which we cling as if it were the main purpose of existence. So many feel that the greater the number of hours they invest in business, the brighter will be the prospects of a successful climb. Even their periods of relaxation overflow with continuing thoughts of how to advance more quickly. Casual strolls with old friends or new acquaintances are frowned upon as a waste of time; an invitation to slow down and ponder other aspects of life is seen as a temptation to avoid the relentless struggle for survival.

God, interested only in eternal gains, gives us time to work and time for leisure. After allowing us six days for toil and labor, He orders us to use the seventh day for rest. Hands busy for a week are expected to fold in prayer. A slowing down on the "day of our Lord" provides calm for rattled nerves and peace to troubled souls. Even when finances pressure our mind, the word of God can always be heard: "Be still and know that I am your Lord." By divine imitation, we are expected to slow down the chase for possessions and focus our inner attention on treasures that "no moth can destroy nor thieves can steal." Our eternal life, infinite yet always approaching, demands an equal share of serious attention. The spiritual dimension, an integral part of every human nature, may lie dormant long before we become aware of its presence. The grace of God dwelling in the very center of our being establishes its own pattern and sanctions. Unless we are sensitive enough to recognize the divine initiations, we could easily assume that God has lost interest in our fate.

The divine milieu is not hostile to human proficiency. Applied in honest motivation, human prowess is an asset in the search for the glory of God. The financial side of life is a necessity, and when business transactions proceed with an awareness of eternal security, they are a value on the scale of human achievement. Haven't saints been recruited from the environment of riches as well as from poverty? If self-indulgence takes first priority, however, the spirit of God may militate against the spirit of the flesh. When physical, mental and spiritual energies are totally consumed with monetary anxieties, when leisure time is not made available for the needs of our soul, a "reevaluation of values" is surely in order.

The belief that science and technology will solve the many problems of mankind is an erroneous assumption. The sum total of happiness becomes questionable when divorced from contemplation and prayer. A paradise filled only with material comforts lacks the spiritual qualities we need to discover inner fulfillment and peace. Only the wisdom of the soul fills us with the strength to become fully alive. An awareness of self-integration at the deepest level of being is evoked not by external possessions but by a commanding sum of spiritual experience and contemplation. Inner stillness, the agent of maturity, often seeks poverty as the most effective medium of expression. Lasting values are never exchanged at a counter.

The mood of the times grants very few favors to our desires for inner tranquility and outer composure. Classified as a transition period from an age of permanence to one of change, the present era demands a variety of quick adjustments, and for this we are not prepared. Our inward journey, however, docile or complicated, has been accustomed to a traditional stride of fulfillment. The ethical norms and moral imperatives that guided many of us to freedom and security were cherished as reliable pointers on our road to God *and* to each other. Eventually, the winds of change turn our well-trusted paths aside, and we find it difficult to recover from the disarray and confusion. Like the Magi of old who did not know where to go when the star disappeared from their sight, we also are confounded by a lack of direction and inspiration.

Experts in behavioral science report that we are less susceptible to disease when we nurture our minds as much as our bodies. Hundreds of cases have been documented in which emotions were shown to have contributed to actual physical disease. Even in a healthy person with a calm and peaceful attitude, anxieties are expected to trigger a chain of events that will affect the brain and endocrine system. This neuroendocrine response is a normal body process, but when emotional upsets are not slowed down and controlled, the physical effects of overstimulation may lead to disease. Research shows that people with tendencies toward depression and anger are more prone to illness than those of a quiet temperament.

Haste and restlessness, so evident in modern life, are accentuated by the widespread inability to relish things in depth. The surface experience, which flatters the cravings of the moment, plays an imperative role in the search for ready-made excitements and sensual gratifications. To flutter from flower to flower rather than enjoying the sight and glory of a particular blossom characterizes much of the modern mentality. Conscious of the fact that the stay here on earth is only temporal, many people dislike the thought of missing any of the passing scene. Those who relentlessly pursue things that they have not yet experienced make themselves unfit for the delight at hand. A vacation planned to relax tensions and strains can turn into a nervous contest of visiting the greatest number of countries in the least amount of days. Arrival at one destination centers on the departure for another; the preparation of setting sails and minds for the next port of call becomes all important. Instead of leisurely enjoying the pleasures and sights at hand, people in a hurry spend time in anticipating excitement that may never come. Unfortunately, the lure of future fields can obscure the satisfaction of the harvest already gathered and destroy our chances for inner harmony and peace.

Today, our popular forms of entertainment seem to make a business of directing our lives. Why do we permit slick television commercials and senseless magazine articles to tell us how to shape our particular life-styles and mode of behavior? Without even thinking, we are swayed by advertisements which claim that success depends on a fascinating job, a picturesque home or an expensive car and diamonds. Should we not know more about our real needs than the invisible advertisers who have never seen us? What has happened to the desire to build our own life as we want it? Those who emulate the frivolities of contemporary living easily sacrifice values that could have been acquired if a more simple style of life had been followed.

Unfortunately many of us, impressed by the speed of an exciting civilization, ignore the tools needed for inner contentment. Vague promises, often not substantiated, take our minds away from the simple master plan that God himself worked out for our final redemption. A sense of natural grace, if allowed to prevail, would indicate most clearly the fulfillment necessary to make our mission on earth meaningful and sacred.

Efforts to bring calm and serenity into life are complicated by stubborn self-reliance and incessant activities. The attitude which insists that we have to do everything ourselves because others cannot be trusted is so stressful that a tranquil life-style is more wish than reality. Work-related travel, long hours at business, and unfinished projects carried home are apt to discourage higher priorities and challenging ideals. Carefully packaged assumptions of fidelity and honor succumb to the relentless pressures of social obligations and material concerns. During a climb to the pinnacle of success, many a self-made man or woman has lost life-sustaining values that money can never replace. A walk alone in silence, an hour of scriptural reading or a time for music or personal development could have prevented the tensions that allowed love to be sacrificed for materialism. "For where your treasure is, there will your heart be also" (Luke 12:34).

Does frail human nature have the resources to cope with an innate, despotic restlessness? Where can the angry and the anxious flee in order to find the elusive calm that a soul needs if it is to grow and deepen? Does history reveal a remedy to cure those who suffer from the enervating fatigue and depletion that capricious living conditions impose on its victims?

In every culture, we find the representatives of God, either self-appointed or inherited, who exist simply to answer the urgent needs of the people. Our Sisters, ministers and priests, with their authenticity and integrity, are an inspiration unmatched by any other effort intended to restore harmony and order. With a dream of God held in their hearts and the message of love on their lips, they are examples of material solicitudes and spiritual priorities that by their very presence induce serenity and peace. The magic formula for holiness is not inherited; it is acquired through a life of prayer. By seeking to experience the death and resurrection of our Lord, religious men and women are in the unique position of opening the way to genuine fulfillment. In union with their Lord and Master, the religious man or woman partakes of a mystery that commands invincible courage and lasting hope. Such disciples of Jesus recognize in this world a kingdom which is not of this world. "They are the ones he chose specially long ago and intended to become true images of his Son" (Rom. 8:29).

Since our leaders of spirituality are formed of the same ordinary clay as the rest of us, they are subjected to the same fragility and weaknesses that we are. Under the pressure of life-styles developed from a rapidly changing world, they too become victimized by the ailments they are attempting to cure. Because they assume an extra share of community responsibilities and greatly extend their working hours, very little time is left for private meditation. In addition to an increase of stress and strain, they soon discover that impatience has become one of their main attributes. And like other compulsive activists, they too are consumed by the same anxieties they were destined to heal. They join the ranks of the infected instead of slowing down and skirting the areas that defile the sacred character of their mission. Troubled waters poorly reflect the beauty of the skies. "Clouds and gusts and yet no rain, such is the man whose promises are princely but never kept" (Prov. 25:14).

Just as Christ gave clear evidence of wrath and anger with the moneychangers in the temple, our spiritual mentors occasionally become disillusioned with their flock. Righteous indignation is indeed fully compatible with the nature of Christian love and human understanding. When dedicated efforts to inspire are frustrated time and again because of human weakness, if the sanctuary becomes a den of thieves and the sacred defiled, the shepherd is bound to bear down on the aberrations of the people. Such reactions are inevitable and should be accepted as a sign of love. But when the fatigue of giving too much changes the personalities of our servants of God, they end up contributing too little. How true the old adage *Cura te ipsum medice*—Heal yourself first, doctor! What a better world it would be if *everyone*, including the ones we depend upon for help, could slow down and reduce the value of push, hurry and run.

Slowing down needs the soothing effect of humor. The person with quick, infectious laughter is well equipped by nature to neutralize the dangerous outbursts of resentment and hasty revenge. A pleasant outlook furnishes the mind and heart with a sanguine outlook on life and encourages the desire to cope with general harassments in a meaningful and light-hearted fashion. Discords arising in relationships with others can be screened by the recuperative powers that see the comical even in the sublime. The buoyant personality reflects a certain mastery over those uncomfortable situations that mar the atmosphere of serenity. Relief from tensions is perhaps the root from which all humor takes its rise.

There are very few emotions that present as many paradoxical contrasts as offered by humor. Hereditary influences and individual experiences determine to a great degree why some people chuckle about a situation over which others shed tears; the same hilarious remark will strike one person with laughter and another with gloom. Next to the spoken word, laughter is the most effective instrument of communication. These stimulating emotions are not always able to manipulate life, but as keen observer of the human condition, they offer everyone the same opportunity to slow anger down and heal the spirit. Medical reports today substantiate the claim that cheerfulness and spontaneous laughter offer significant therapeutic value. "Go, eat your bread with joy and drink your wine with a glad heart" (Eccles. 9:7).

Sufferings, failures, or inner enlightenment teach us to cherish values that are not transitory but are of everlasting worth. Superficial causes that consume the energies and capacities of our youth usually lose their attraction when compared with experiences involved with more inspiring and higher goals of life. Only when the frantic pace of life yields to quiet, reflective thought is the mind willing to "slow down." Such an effort may arise from our own initiative or it may be occasioned by the hidden impulses of the Divine Spirit. "Riches" lying within the heart prompt a more fervent response than the excitement of momentary prosperity. Treasures that never lose value become the new investment. Because we are no longer interested in being what others expect us to become, we are able to seek peace in ourselves.

Our Lord once commanded belligerent waves to slow down, to be still; according to the Word, the stormy sea listened obediently and smoothed its angry face into peaceful submission. Confronted with similar upheavals, we too possess a magical strength that enables us to slow down our personal storms with a spirit of calmness. The powerful resource called inner stillness alleviates many of the effects that haste and turmoil impose on our frayed nerves. By permeating every corner of our soul, inner calm and quiet keep our restless ambitions within the realm of our capacities and wisdom. We learn to assess our potential in order to measure our deeds. In slowing down, we grasp the meaning of humility.

Today, perhaps more than ever before, quiet time is needed to interrupt the anxious hours and provide a period of rest so that new ideas can be born and better worlds can develop. Just as religious leaders first sought solitude before they proclaimed their message, we also can discover stillness to help us perfect our thoughts. Unless we reserve a place in our hearts for all that is good, honest and true, the magnificence of the universe will be curtailed with the selfish measures of our deeds. Only when our souls find tranquility and peace in the midst of turmoil and destruction will we perceive the wisdom of an ageless past.

Chapter 3

MORALITY

Morality is losing pace
And few have questioned why;
Unless the faithful take a stand
The world will pass us by.

Sometimes when morality is discussed, people seem reticent to offer a real opinion because they are not sure which direction the subject will take. Occasionally, some of the listeners will gather courage and confess that even though they know all about it, they are lost when it comes to explaining what morality is and where it can be found. An old man may complain that times were good when morality was around: "We weren't afraid to leave our doors open because everyone was trustworthy, but now people are frightened and prefer to remain home at night with their rooms securely locked." A young person, however, will seize the opportunity to voice personal disagreement: "I do not miss morality at all. I need to do as I please and no one can change my mind. All this talk about honesty and goodness is foolish nonsense." A middle-aged character unwilling to expose definite ideas on morality will take the neutral stance until one of the given opinions gets the upper hand. Then the uncommitted voice will join the winning side, not because it is convincing, but because that is the best way to avoid a real confrontation with truth. In following others, it is easy to dispense with the scrutiny of self.

What has happened to morality? Is it still around or has a leave of absence been taken because it no longer feels welcomed by the present generation? Perhaps morality has left our surroundings for other places where its appearance is more appreciated! How long has it been since remarkable numbers of people strongly believed that morality was destined to play a significant role in our public and private lives? In the past, the desire to act with truth and responsibility was not the exception; it was the only way to live. A promise given was a promise kept; vows exchanged were sacred obligations. Anyone who failed to live up to the highest expectations was ostracized by friends and shunned by acquaintances. Jobs were jeopardized whenever an immoral infraction embarrassed an employer. To sympathize with the offender was almost as serious as participating in the deed. Immorality was shocking and decent men or women refused to take part in it.

Unfortunately, times have changed, and with the times, some of our convictions changed, too. The "unacceptable" of yesterday is more readily accepted today. Without noticeable resistance from the average person, indecent and vulgar attitudes move up on the ladder of propriety. Standards of behavior previously not sanctioned are allowed to exist now without question. Actions once decidedly private are now publicly discussed; unmentionable words of a bygone era are part of open and daily usage. The pure mingles with the impure as if each were similar in value.

It is true, of course, that public laws continue to judge impartially the civility of our citizens; many criminals are caught and deprived of their freedom. Strangers are willing to help others in need, and our freely elected government functions in a fairly efficient manner. Liberty, still our greatest heritage, heads the list of the many things for which we are grateful.

Regulations, however, govern only the outer conduct of the people. Public actions that affect the common good are scrutinized, not the inner motivation. The core of our being where good and evil rest is not conditioned by the written statute alone. To encourage youth to strive for excellence and to inspire people to pursue their goals require much more than judicial or legal commands. Convictions of virtue are meaningful and supported only when deeply imbedded in the human heart. And surely, if we believe that moral demands reveal a divine wish, we will want to obey. Education that stresses religious and honest values deserves "top priority" in our teaching as well as in our learning. The conscientious citizen will always be our most formidable line of defense against the invasion of degenerate ideals. To allow the looseness of customs and habits to destabilize long-cherished traditions and obligations undermines not only the lifestyle of the present but also the development of the future. Military strength provides little security if it is not disciplined and ruled by sincerity and truth.

Studies of the evolution of human behavior describe us as barbarians long before we became civilized. Culture is not an inborn, unchangeable capacity of the growing personality. Aesthetic tastes and artistic tendencies are cultivated by traditional training and exposure to other people and places. In years gone by, men and women were eager and ready to improve their manner of living whenever they were exposed to more civilized patterns of behavior. Whether through the influence of Christianity or a constant inner surge of self-improvement, individuals gradually aspired to a *modus vivendi*, a life-style that proved superior to their own. Today our own cultural fulfillments have by no means reached their ultimate heights. We also are always in need of being present to the achievements of others in order to improve our own concept of how to experience life at its fullest.

No one is *born* good; it is up to each one of us to *become* good. We are what we make ourselves to be. In matters of moral certitude and ethical decisions, some of us may be more ignorant than we like to admit. Latent weaknesses or obvious painful inclinations remind us of our frailties the very moment we think we are above reproach. After all, the warning of Christ to call no one good but your heavenly Father must apply most of all to ourselves. Those who seriously live their beliefs of integrity and honesty are the ones who can give our youth the best help.

To expect moral discipline to restore itself is to miscalculate the power and cunning of evil. Misdeeds in various forms and addictions have spread so far and wide that no one remains immune to the effects. Everyone has the choice of remaining blind to the magnitude of this threat or of confronting the danger with the intention of slowing down the spread. An education that disregards personal ideals and respect for others is a poor preparation for the eventual resurrection of values.

Fear suggested gently and with reason exerts a beneficial influence in the growth of a human being. Guidelines enforced save many a young life from tragic error. Modern educators have a tendency to look upon "salutary fear" as an unworthy inducement for achieving success. In their opinion, personal motivation without threat of punishment provides the most efficient stimulus for the desire to excel. Such idealism would be justified for the flawless and pure personality, but real life reveals dimensions that are in stark contrast to such innocence and sinlessness. Selfishness and pride without healthy correctives would soon establish their own rules of self-worship and egotism. "Do as you please" may be tempting to the *one* but it can be most disastrous for the *many*. Impressive records have not yet been established by the philosophy of education that ignores the therapeutic value of fear.

A major flaw in the makeup of people is a total lack of consistency in their convictions. Attitudes toward moral absolutes rise and fall according to the tune of the latest fad. Purity and faithfulness have been demeaned by the current mode of couples who live together without paying heed to religious responsibilities and obligations. Chastity, the resolve of the strong, is instantly labeled "neurotic." Honesty is kept on a pedestal as long as it remains self-serving. Promiscuity, so rampant today, is discussed as one of the possible ways of adjusting to modern conditions. Morality is seldom invited to play its natural role in the practical settle-

ment of life's predicaments. Bystanders, even though not actually involved in these new experiences, show support when
they cover themselves with silence and passive submission.

Freedom of choice is still a treasured privilege. No one is
coerced into attending questionable performances, nor are
television productions of sexual exploitations forced onto our
screens. But why should our freedoms be tested in such lewd
fashion? The "flock" is in dire need of a good shepherd to
provide inspiration and guidance. Why are some people allowed to curse while others are forbidden to pray? Those
who lack the ability to think clearly and find it difficult to
distinguish between pasture and poisonous weed must remain open to the guidance offered by dedicated teachers,
counselors and religious directors. Our youth especially, so
vulnerable and easily misled by the ethos of our times, are
frontline victims of peddlers of the cheap and erotic. How
could we have allowed a civilization to develop in which it
is impossible for children to grow up in innocence? Isn't this
one of our greatest sins? And adding to the problem is the
fact that very little is being done to reverse this pernicious
trend. Are enough of us asking "Where will it end?"

A strong, hostile power that militates against morality is
the dominance we attach to material values. External fortunes overshadow internal riches. Economic laws that rule
our society demand profits which in return establish their
own regulations of influence and greed. The *more* subdues
inhibitions about the *how*. The desire to produce the greatest
financial return in the shortest period of time condones actions not always in full accord with integrity and honor. More
than one conscience is victimized by the insatiable hunger
for greater benefits and gains. Not that affluence itself is in
conflict with morality; some individuals of wealth strive sincerely to obey moral injunctions. But the magnetic force that
wealth exudes dims a sensitivity for the importance of spiritual needs. A mind set exclusively on worldly success finds
little time or energy left to pursue the value of the spirit.
Few financial tycoons would agree that poverty, which is
honest, is more desirable than wealth, which is question-

able. Profits earned by the industrious hand are justified; profits that accrue because of personal position lend themselves to criticism and doubt. "Happy the rich man who is found to be blameless and does not go chasing after gold" (Eccles. 31:8).

Inner harmony, not material wealth, is the key to real inner fulfillment. Ideals that lead the imagination beyond the horizon of the visible offer challenges of greater importance than the accumulation of possessions. Fidelity to a promise made ennobles our character much more than loyalty to financial gains. The growing disenchantment with a life in which wealth becomes an all-consuming passion proves that the soul yearns for much more than things. We must cling to the hope that our rebellious youth will search for experiences that transcend the whole scale of materialism without the use of drugs.

Lessons taught by poverty supersede lessons conveyed by way of affluence. When we share the little we have with others, it is not just a gift that is presented by a giving of ourselves. How meaningful the things we offer to others, how empty the things when we keep them ourselves. As stewards of God's treasures on earth, we have a right to the reasonable means of providing for our sustenance. This right, however, includes the obligation of helping to alleviate, from our surplus, the woes of the less fortunate. When things given away are considered a loss, the joy of sharing is not experienced and the gift is wasted. Only when happiness on the face of the receiver remains our greatest reward have we mastered the art of giving. A gift to the other returns as a gift to self.

Morality gathers little acclaim in our modern world. Old-fashioned rules are not favorably regarded by the self-indulgent because such directives curb the uninhibited expression of desire. If everyone acted in behalf of personal pleasure alone, without regard for others, the civilized way of living would soon be a relic of the past. The rights of the *many* must find a common ground with the right of the *one*. Although the *other* can never be considered more important that the *self*, it should always equal the self. The needs and fulfillment of both complement each other. These who have found their own identity relate without difficulty. Those who are still in search of self face long periods of struggle in order to reach out with sincerity. Anyone who is a problem to self becomes a problem to others.

The ability to uphold principles without appearing objectionable demands strong convictions and endless patience. Friction and misunderstandings due to various interpretations of values are the inevitable characteristics of life. Anyone who allows sameness to determine personal choices and judgments merely adds another stone to the already heavy load of boredom. Variety becomes a delight when it is greeted with joy and satisfaction. As long as contradictory opinions stir up feelings of rejection, we are not mature and free enough to engage in meaningful dialogue. It is when we grant others the right to think through their own ideas that channels to a profound human relationship of respect are kept open. Fellowship grows deeper when it does not inhibit different perceptions. Love that demands intellectual and emotional agreement is based not on genuine affection but on the desire to dominate.

Some of us adjust to our moral obligations more readily than others. What is it that makes one person receptive to ethical imperatives while another feels the need to refuse? Experiences in the early stages of life provide a decisive answer to this question. When truth, honesty and respect permeate the atmosphere of family life, the inner growth of the child is deeply affected. If love is experienced, love is kept alive. Honesty lived inspires the continuing urge to imitate. Early adventures, joyous or painful, cut deep furrows into the soil of youth, especially in the early years when the stage is set for the shape of future events. The young mirror the faces of the old. Education alone, even when perfectly adjusted to the child's abilities and functions, cannot make up for the damages inflicted on the abandoned child. Effects of apathy and rejection linger on, asserting themselves in moments least expected. The misdeeds of people are in the making long before the actual event occurs.

At the outset of life a child's potentials are waiting to be developed. Life is latent and needs to be parentally nourished and guided. Responsibility usually develops gradually with the use of reflection and reasoning. The function of any wise educator is to direct the student with patience in the search for freedom and knowledge. Possessiveness, indifference or extreme expectations lead to unbalanced growth. Children become rebellious when too much is demanded of them just as maturity will suffer if too little is asked.

A person who intends to live within the divine code of morality cannot always endorse the prevailing opinions regarding right and wrong. The secular ethos tries to impose a variety of decisions that are bound to be unacceptable to the believer. The Christian must be able to distinguish laws that are in accord with the dictates of the conscience and laws that are in direct violation of moral priorities. Some aspects of our present culture can be gratefully accepted; however, when such rules of conduct and binding customs alter the divine command, there is no choice to be made . . . the Christian must refuse. "Make no mistake about this, my dear brothers: it is all that is good, everything that is perfect, which is given us from above; it comes down from the Father of all light; with him there is no such thing as alteration, no shadow of a change" (James 1:16–17).

In our dâily motivations we are guided either by powers from within or by authorities from without. Since we are primarily "spirit oriented," we need to return time and again to the supernatural sources to keep our priorities balanced. As social beings, we are also subject to the mandates of civil authorities. A compliance with public ordinances is not only an exterior function, it is also an interior response from a conscience-bound individual. Only when fidelity to public decrees is purely servile, without any reference to a love for the spirit of God, is submission unworthy of human dignity and honor. The moment we bow to orders issued by authorities purely because of fear, we act without integrity and freedom. Often the law of the state is in concordance with the divine intention. Even Christ urged us to give to Caesar what is due Caesar and to give to God what is due to God.

Caution, of course, must be used whenever there is a conflict of values.

In the Old Testament, the path to salvation is not so strictly defined as we would like. In the New Testament, however, our journey is eased with the teachings and examples of Christ. His life on earth marks our way to heaven. Human as our Savior was, He went through the same series of trials and tribulations that confront us today. Whenever we struggle over our periods of misfortunes, we can take strength and courage from a Master who already suffered through similar circumstances. He was "one of us" in everything except sin.

In searching for answers to our moral problems, we can rely on the voice of God speaking within us through the spiritual gift of conscience. Divine wisdom recognized can readily become wisdom lived. Participating in this wisdom and feeling God's presence within the core of our being prepares us to adjust our moral activities to the voice that speaks within our soul. Such an adjustment differs in intensity and gradation according to the sensitivity of our talents. For some of us, conscience is the inner responsibility toward the needs of the community; others believe it is right insight into what is really good; a few consider conscience an inner power founded on the order of love. And of course there are those who look upon conscience as the faculty that allows us to discern the call of God and to follow without hesitation.

Circumstances conditioned by upbringing, environment and relationships deeply influence the way our conscience awakens and grows. By doing things rightly or by correcting things poorly done, we demonstrate that our inner voice is asserting itself with clarity and conviction. Those who succeed in integrating inner mandates with outer performance prove that conscience is not only a dry and abstract principle but a very real living process. When justice, love and truth are endangered, people guided by moral values strongly defend these ancient principles. By consistently promoting and nurturing an attitude of ethical values and aesthetic standards, we enforce the roots from which our conscience takes its growth.

Much of our present moral confusion stems from the fact that people are showered with words that are never followed by deeds.

Many of us respect what our "inner Master" commands, but not all of us are willing to cope with the consequences of His words. There are so many times when we know what has to be done and yet we refuse to do it. Since the word of God invites, never coerces, it is up to us to listen and respond. When we nod in approval, the festival concept of life triumphs; when we resist and decline, God turns aside with sadness. Although our Lord loves us and desires to see us advance with giant strides along the paths of His love, He does not want this to happen at the expense of our freedom. He grants us liberty to do whatever we like until the end of our lives. Whether or not we build our human existence on the ideas that God had at the moment of our creation or shape our destiny without the grace of the Divine is a decision for each one of us to make alone.

A PARABLE

There was once a man who had a dream, and so we'll call him the Dreamer. As dreams go, this one was not a pleasant one. It began with a strangely vivid scene that featured a procession marching along a fog-enshrouded avenue to the local graveyard. The mourners appeared emotionally moved but not overwrought with grief. Eager to find out more about the funeral, the Dreamer joined the line of people, stepping in by the side of a small, white-haired woman.

"Can you tell me, please, who is being buried here today?" he whispered. "Is it a man, woman or child?"

"No one like that," she answered sharply. After hesitating for a moment, she looked up and spoke again.

"It is not a person they are putting away, it is a thing, a real thing!"

"What do you mean?" the Dreamer replied in puzzlement. "What kind of thing?"

"Well," the lady whispered, "they called it Goodness, I guess, or Morality. It was around for a long time, but now no one seems to care about it anymore!"

Intrigued with her comments, he became very interested in the people around him. He noticed that all of them wore a distinctive badge on the lapels of their dark clothes. Some of the badges were lettered *liberal* and others had the word *conservative*. Although the difference in behavior between the two groups was very slight, the *liberals* appeared more relaxed than the *conservatives*. The Dreamer, not able to decide which side he preferred, edged toward the sidelines until the line approached the gate of the burial grounds. With a clear view of the proceedings, he watched the casket being lowered and the members paying their last respects. A question weighed heavily on the Dreamer's mind. What difference would it make to a Morality laid to rest if it were interred by a *liberal* or a *conservative*? As he turned around in order to leave the grounds, his attention was drawn to a gravedigger standing nearby.

"I worry," the old worker muttered as he leaned on his shovel. "I worry about us all. How easy to get rid of Morality, but how hard to live without it!"

Moved by such a frightful thought, the Dreamer sat on the ground by the side of the road and searched his heart for the answer. Suddenly, before he could put his thoughts into words, the music of the processional band leaving the graveyard echoed in his ears and awakened him.

If you were the Dreamer, what would your answer be?

Chapter 4

EXCELLENCE

I strive and seek perfection,
I live without pretense;
My soul is set in discipline—
They call me excellence.

The most valuable and desirable resource of a country is the wisdom and intelligence of its people. Citizens noted for their mental prowess and artistic vitality are a greater asset than military valor or economic might. History abounds with many examples which prove that nations poor in natural resources have achieved a civilized standard of living because they knew how to cultivate creativity and excellence in their people. A government that extends priorities to values fashioned by the human mind lays claim to immortality long after its heroes have gone. How different are the memories we have of Hitler and Stalin when compared to those we have of Plato, Aristotle, Einstein or Beethoven! In the short view of life it might be physical prowess that is the most impressive; yet in the long view the intellectual or spiritual masterpiece is the one that endures. A nation that tolerates or even fosters an educational system that brings forth a number of barely literate students lays waste its greatest potential, the mind of its youth. Remove the challenge and mediocrity is born; glorify banality and the possibilities awaiting discovery face merciless extinction. The moment the lowest denominator of life is made a common standard, inspirations of human

greatness are banished from the realm of our national con-
sciousness. The impossible dream has to be kept fully alive
in the imagination and realization of our present generation.
Fortunately the most difficult missions on earth continue to
attract the interests of our most dedicated men and women.

Excellence never rests on the previous level of accomplishments. What is now known is infinitely less than what is
not yet known. The scientific appetite considers the mysteries unrevealed as a welcome shadow on the horizon, a
temptation leading to new discoveries and exciting inventions. Twice we have to become strangers: once to the desire
to be content with our triumphs, and once to the fiction that
we have already achieved our best. Learning is a lifelong
task. When we prematurely terminate our desires to discover and advance, we draw the curtain on wonder and awe.
The claim that we know enough points to the possibility that
we perceive too little.

The first Paradise was created by God and we spoiled it;
the second paradise, our comfort zone, was created by ourselves and we allowed it to spoil us. The warmth of a shelter, the security of the roof, the opulent provisions we enjoy
tend to exert such a dominant influence upon our concerns
and actions that everything else becomes subject to their
command. Like a prison, the comfort zone holds us captive
and stifles the freedom needed to react quickly and deci-
sively to other exigencies and predicaments. Inertia, the most
pernicious frustration of excellence, flourishes in living conditions that are affluent yet boring. The powers of vision
and the will to excel are better served by discipline than by
a life-style of total freedom. When given too much, human
nature cares too little. Pampered youth sow our land with
graves in which potential heroes are laid to rest. The most
beautiful gift a parent can offer a child is the courage of not
giving it everything.

We get more satisfaction from doing a good job than from
admiring the finished product. To follow through, to carry
out, to try again interests us as much as the glorious ending
of the great adventure. The *how* of the incredible feat of con-

quering the moon brought more excitement to the human genius than the actual landing itself. Mental alertness and emotional stability are the precious foundations upon which the tower of success can be secured. Some of us look, others applaud, a few do nothing; those born to succeed usually reach out for every opportunity and strive for a fruitful conclusion. A number of people are born leaders and others have to be trained; whatever the origin of leadership, there is little difference in the determination to assume full responsibility for deeds and omissions. Political and social principles are announced not to flatter the taste of the public but to serve as a moral beacon for our attitudes and behavior. Overeagerness to compromise reveals a character far too dependent upon the opinions of others. To stand fearlessly on top of a mountain in support of one's humble decision reflects a self-confidence that renders assurance to friends and a warning to foes. The rudders of the skiff are in stable hands when the captain of the journey charts the course with determination and courage. A resolute will can turn defeat into a stunning victory, whereas the fearful and hesitant take to flight even when success is within sight. Those without a goal in life choose any road in sight; others, convinced of their mission, will walk the one road and follow it to the end.

To feel responsible is to experience the power of God. We sense shame when we tangle with betrayal and are embarrassed when we shift our burdens onto others. From where do emotions of this kind, robbing us of our sleep, our peace and our honor, arise? Surely not from ourselves, because we hate such feelings; it takes a higher power to plant the seed of responsibility in our arid souls. If individual actions are to accompany us into the world yet to come, our most responsible deeds will surely rank the highest in the account we are expected to render.

We need courage in order to follow a course with fearlessness and discipline. Conflicts between inner and outer signals mix black and white into an indistinguishable gray. Ethical values, for centuries our guide and protection, begin to tremble the very moment we need their support. Confusion surrounding the doctrines of Church and nation make us suspicious regarding the validity of right and wrong concepts. Parents attempting to educate their offspring lament the lack of guidance from those eternal sources of morality that previously provided the beacons of light. Today, faith, honor and glory are allowed to speak with so many different voices that listeners everywhere become hapless victims of uncertainties.

Present-day freedoms entice people to throw responsibility overboard and continue with whatever pleases them the most. Those who make such a callous choice in life have to live with the consequences of their decisions. The ones who go to the source of inspiration in search of answers to their perplexities find their greatest consolation as they seek the better solution. It is doubtful that our present generation will see the arrival of the new vision; doesn't the seed have to fall into the furrow and die before a new harvest can be expected? In the meantime, all of us have an obligation to preserve the well-being of the world simply because it is the only world we know. As long as sincerity remains our chief delight, progress can be expected.

Nothing is so insecure as security. Our infallible weapons system has failed; unsinkable ships lie helpless on the floor of the oceans; foolproof bank vaults are rifled at random by common thieves. Even if every human promise were carried out to perfection, Mother Earth would spoil our bliss with fires, drought and a variety of calamities in order to teach us that we are *not* the masters of our destiny.

When individual patterns of inner security are minimal or nonexistent, the person born to excel is able to act by calling on the source of courage. Self-confidence and faith become the substitute factors when, because of this insecurity, there is an absence of certitude. The first flight over the ocean and the first successful climb of the highest mountain were achieved by daring men who totally disregarded their security and trusted in their abilities to face reasonable risks. The prayer "God help me" is often the outcry of men and women who realize that when left to their own strength and commitment they might never reach total fulfillment. Rarely are such words uttered by people who think that *they* are in full command of their powers. Fortunately, we are never totally dependent on ourselves. Even when human safeguards collapse, the will and intellect still function; our strength is rooted not only in daring but also in the wonder of belief.

Creative inspirations offer themselves in proportion to a person's intellectual and emotional maturity. Messages are understood according to the perception of the receiver. Since success usually depends on being fully alerted to the exciting moment when greatness knocks at the door, writers, artists, poets and even the average man, woman and child determined to excel try to keep themselves in a state of readiness. As long as the mind is not fatigued or abused by the clatter of banalities, it is free to respond to the inspirations that a future masterpiece evokes in the imagination. By rehearsing mentally over and over again what they are going to write, to sing, to dance, to create or to say, people tuned into the melody and drama of success will work with continuing interest. Procrastinators and sleepers who mull over what they are *going* to do seldom find the enthusiasm and time ever to get it done. The idea of triumph and defeat is not a game as some imply; it is more a hard-earned reward or result of earnest work and fearlessness. Like nature, excellence needs many storms and seasons to ripen and mature.

The desire to excel has to be protected from its own means of destruction. What is noble in the beginning can become ignoble in the end. However well meant, the eagerness to exceed, to prevail and to outrival others can be so intense and ruthless that values of decency and honor are totally obliterated. To allow a particular and unbreakable attachment to seize control of our spirit will stunt the growth of our feelings toward the rights of other human beings. In the end, only those who are free interiorly and exteriorly from compulsion and coercion will ascend to the level where greatness is born. People who are not endowed with creativity are easily tempted to make a sacred ritual of any status quo. The disaster zone of life is crowded with individuals who suffer when confronted with new ideas. Boring repetitions will be the only heritage they bequeath to their youth if echoes of the past replace ingenuity and originality. The language of yesterday does not increase the quality of today's capacity to listen. Priests and ministers are not urged to accept fully the mentality of our times—that would make them puppets instead of redeemers—but we have a right to expect our clergy and counselors to study the motivations of our civilization in order to redeem it from its fallacies. Ignorance alone is fatal.

After many, many trials, the determined actions of our ancestors succeeded in constructing the wheel; this was an early historical achievement of importance. Since then, the human genius has traveled astonishing roads of discovery that led to the amazing landing on the moon. And who can predict what the future will hold? Dramatic as this progress may be, we are not wholly convinced that our spiritual values or moral convictions are truly enriched by these material advances. It is possible for those of us born in these periods of scientific triumphs to be openly exposed to knowledge and yet remain totally closed to inner evaluation. Although the challenge of past discoveries can be extremely valuable, it is equally important that we challenge our youngsters to grow in courage, respect and responsibility. To promote the "outside" without intensifying the "inside" ignores the most consequential part of the human structure.

Profanities and superficialities have infiltrated the fields of entertainment and modern literature to such a disturbing extent that we find ourselves reduced from aesthetic highs to the most embarrassing lows. People are so accustomed to social misadventures and glorified mediocrities that experiences of shame are reduced to laughter instead of criticism. The mind, destined by divine wisdom to bear the royal purple in God's brilliant creation, occasionally clothes itself in rags in order to disguise its lack of originality, novelty and freshness. Instead of drawing inspiration from the reservoir of faith, self-denial, triumphs and failures, the mentality dependent on financial gain returns to the human underbrush to replenish its sources of supply. How can we expect the elite of our youth to peer through the holes of deception and *not* sense the emptiness of our culture!

The dream of excellence, however, will never vanish. A resurrection of values is always within the reach of humanity as a whole, within the grasp of the individual gazing at the firmament, searching for the stars. The outcry of the Apostles, "He is risen!" is a sacred command to those of us who have eyes to see, ears to hear and the capacity to understand the implications of our deeds. A wonderful grace rests upon our souls, the grace to put behind us what is unworthy of our mission on earth. By directing our inner powers with a disciplined mind and a loving heart, we may be capable of creating that masterpiece of excellence that will be applauded and admired by our own generation and by all generations to come as well.

Chapter 5

COMPASSION

To refuse my hand
To strengthen another,
Is to question God's wisdom
And dismiss my Brother.

Compassion is that particular orientation in the human character that responds sympathetically to the pains and exaltations of life. Not exactly a religion in itself, it is an integral part of every religious sentiment and feeling. It contains a full measure of the spiritual and material worlds, both of which are part of our earthly heritage. Divine love and human affections blend into one powerful emotion.

Universal by nature, compassion reaches beyond the range of friends and neighbors. Unfortunate strangers are entitled to our loving attention just as much as people who are part of our lives. When the timeless figure of the Good Samaritan stopped to care for someone he had never known before, the uniting element was not the personal relationship but the human need. And to this day, anyone struggling for survival should be considered more of a friend than a stranger.

There is a destiny that brings us all together. Whatever we contribute to insure the survival of others is also invested in the survival of ourselves. Altruistic as compassion is, it also serves our self-interest in a good way. Being part of the network of giving and receiving, we realize that what one person suffers today can hurt us similarly tomorrow, putting us in need of help. No one can make it alone. One day we lead, the next day we may follow. Whereas philosophers interpret the world according to different concepts, people of compassion reduce all experiences to one mandate: to suffer with those who are suffering.

The goal of the pilgrimage on earth is not personal happiness alone. Time and energy spent in lightening another person's burdens are not only pure expressions of sympathy but can also be essential factors in the final shape of our destiny. Religious motivations as much as moral convictions enable us to seek contentment in the joy and satisfaction we provide to others. When we share ourselves, the horizons of the receiver are widened and our own understanding of humanity is deepened. People of an unsympathetic nature who celebrate life alone in their hearts condemn themselves to a narrowness that impoverishes their viewpoint. Isolated from love, the main purpose of life, they seek consolation in material fortune as the answer to all their needs.

Compassion, sustained by feelings of warmth and togetherness, is threatened by a prevailing bureaucracy that performs corporal acts of mercy with efficiency and coldness. Although the old, the sick and the helpless are cared for most competently in many of our professional homes, the atmosphere is sometimes one of neutrality and indifference. In such places no one dies of hunger or suffers from a lack of care or medicine, but something is missing in the long and lonely corridors of human misery and torment; something has been lost in the complicated shuffle of laws and regulations. Isn't this "something" the love that every human being needs to feel better? Without this love and without compassion, even the best institution can provide little more than material necessities. Without this love and without compassion, not much can be done to alleviate loneliness and frustration. Provisions distributed without affection feed the body and starve the heart. If hospitality extends only to physical needs, the real hunger of every human being is left unattended. Only when sustenance is dispensed with understanding and endearment is the body nourished and the cry of the soul stilled.

Pity is similar in appearance to compassion but differs in its motivations and goals. Compassion is stirred into prompt and healing action whenever it is confronted with tribulation, whereas pity communicates the sympathetic sentiment without exerting itself and without stepping beyond the limits of carefully guarded comforts. Usually, pity contains traces of condescension or feelings of superiority when it looks upon the person in distress not only as a victim of suffering but also as one personally responsible for the problem. Unlike compassion, which recognizes that someday it may suffer the other person's distress, pity gloats over the fact that the distress belongs to someone else. Compassion comes as a friend; pity leaves as a stranger.

Even when accompanied with tears, sentiments expressed in words alone do not guarantee effective relief for our suffering friends. Our aroused emotions of sympathy spend themselves so quickly that nothing is accomplished unless our determined will forces us into action. In order for us to comfort the afflicted, to instruct the ignorant, and to counsel people in doubt, we need to be calm and cool under the pressures of anguish and torment. Usually, the person in need counts on deeds of relief, not on a show of sympathetic attention. "If a man who was rich enough in this world's goods saw that one of his brothers was in need, but closed his heart to him, how could the love of God be living in him?" (1 John 3:17).

The distress and misfortunes of other people sharpen our sensitivities for sincerity and truth. The camouflage we so often employ to hide our real feelings has no place in the room of the sick. When confronted with illness, both the sufferer and the observer have to show emotions that are real and honest. Any pretense, however conventional and soothing, brings little lasting comfort. The patient cleansed by pain quickly recognizes the counterfeit.

Compassion, so eager to mirror deeds, has to assume an occasional silence in order to reach the tortured heart. Physical and mental injuries often affect the body so seriously that words can only intensify the discomfort. A silent presence fulfills the demand of the moment; to be there lifts the terrible suspicion that the suffering friend will be abandoned and left alone. Offering our prayers, our hands and the nearness of our person create the most moving moments in the rich history of compassion. Our own sensitivity and imagination will clearly reveal the immediate needs. Further demonstrations of commiseration would be superfluous. Real love never has to search for the time to speak and the time to fall back into silence. Genuine affection will determine the right moment and the right choice of words.

Owing to its surprising versatility, compassion is as much at ease with joy as it is with sorrow. Since tears and laughter make up the common lot of people, compassion must always remain an adaptable guest. Both rejoicing and sympathizing have to find a cherished spot in our affections. For the mature person, sadness and gladness are simply different expressions of the whole latitude of the human condition. Light and darkness exact a response in an individual existence just as they did in the life of Christ. Men and women who are conscious of the splendor and shadows of fate are well prepared to endure both without undue agitation. The immature, however, who have never learned to bear with disappointment will quickly be ravaged by inevitable destructive elements. Life remains a friend to those who know how to deal with enemies.

The way we treat people reflects clearly the standards of our ethical and religious convictions. If we praise some of them for their good looks and despise others for their poor appearance, our judgments are based not on inner values but on the imagined show of glamour. Ideals we believe in are apt to be overshadowed by exterior factors that have little to do with inner worth. If people in authority adopt a moral scale of values in which power and fortune rank supreme, what chances for success are left to the poor and the hopeless? When power is used to make them powerless, power itself is indicted. Competition as an incentive is valuable; when used as an aggressive force to eliminate the weak, it becomes a tool of the unscrupulous. A society which implies that only the mighty shall survive deserves to be eliminated.

Wealth and compassion are not necessarily hostile to each other; neither of the two possesses tendencies that are mutually exclusive. Riches honestly acquired and administered produce many benefits from which others less fortunate draw support and relief. Although money undoubtedly causes a variety of evils, the lack of it often terminates much good. In themselves, material possessions are morally neutral. Fortunes, it has been said, have no religion, but surely they can become a substitute religion by exercising control over mental and spiritual convictions. If people born into a milieu of luxury are fair-minded and compassionate, they will not have to be taught how to use their riches. Their own sense of responsibility and integrity will chart the course of mind and heart into the right direction. Anyone who considers wealth a private domain and is not concerned for the poor creates a feeling of hate that can threaten the existence of us all. To be victimized by the greed of people who consciously violate the sacred demands of justice is not only unfair, it is also totally inhuman. "Treasures wickedly come by give no benefit, but right conduct brings delivery from death" (Prov. 10:2).

If compassion were permitted to nurture favorites, youth would be singled out to receive special attention. Born into a civilization in which it seems impossible to grow up in innocence, our young people are beset by temptations to which we were seldom exposed. Mind-altering drugs, habit-forming barbiturates and easy money lure our boys and girls into sensuous activities that destroy their souls and bodies. Not yet fully aware of the difference between good and evil, young people succumb to evil as if it were good. Little, far too little, is being done to prevent greedy merchants from making this helpless group their favorite ploy. Even our classrooms, previously proud citadels of learning, can be turned into pits of mire and perdition. In the name of freedom that now has become license, honest efforts for redeeming actions are stymied and perversities are left free to roam. How unfortunate that the one thing which is prohibited is the freedom of speaking to students about the love of God.

If we are disappointed with the moral character of some of our youth, we should ask ourselves who permitted the present environment to come into existence. Was it the work of the younger generation or of the adults who preceded them? Haven't we, the older generation, contributed to the dilemma by remaining silent when we should have spoken? Aren't we all conspirators if with open eyes we pretend a blindness to the problems? When we place the blame on our younger generation without accepting our share of the guilt, we continue to ignore our responsibilities as adults and leaders. Many of the calamities faced today by our children began in times and situations when we were in a position to reverse the trend. "Fight to the death for truth, and the Lord God will war on your side" (Eccles. 4:28).

Fortunately, compassion thrives on the knowledge of solidarity. What the other person did, we might also have done had our circumstances been the same. Maybe our situation favored us more and we were not caught for similar misdemeanors. Perhaps the fact that our parents have been more loving and our education a little better made the difference between decency and disgrace. The offspring welcomed with affection experiences delight; the child cursed and unwanted rebels. If the "why" of violence were known, some of the publicized violent deeds would cease to shock us. Blatant injustices, hurt sensitivities suppressed too long break out in a most terrifying manner. The wounded human animal can plot revenge more viciously than the animal in the forest. When compassion succeeds in bringing light and truth to a distorted view of life, it has achieved a remarkable triumph.

By its very nature, compassion prefers to be modest and reserved in its manner of appearance. Thoughts that give solace and deeds that bring relief are most effective when presented without expected returns. Gifts offered with the blare of trumpets embarrass the receiver. Love can be very sincere even when not demonstrative. Mercy advertised is vanity concealed. Compassion remains most efficient when it can withdraw the moment the wounded have found their own power of healing. Human sympathy overextended is in

danger of becoming a meaningless gesture, but genuine sorrow offered as an evidence of faith can be as comfortable on
the sidelines as it is in the center of events. When compassion is used as a means of satisfying personal aspirations,
the misfortunes of others are easily forgotten.

The heart of the poor is the favorite place for compassion
to establish residence. The unfortunate ones are always willing to help out those who have less than they. Having little
themselves, they are familiar with the humiliations that poverty brings. An opportunity to spare others such feelings
brings them pleasure and they are generous beyond their
means. The poor see in the beggar the most wonderful chance
to give like a king. Whatever they own becomes so much
more when shared with people who have nothing. Those
with few possessions and riches in their hearts are the most
attractive and important members of our human family.

People who care only for themselves miss the intense
gratification of being generous. How poor the soul who has
never experienced the exquisite joy that is returned after we
have given something to someone. To love only oneself, and
selfishly, is not to love at all; to love ourselves in the loving
of others obeys God's greatest command. God assures us
that the more liberal we are in distributing our gifts, the more
ample will be the rewards.

Usually, women possess a greater capacity for compassion
than men. Owing to the woman's extremely sensitive feelings for human nature, her emotions respond well to the
cries of "life in distress." To care and to cure are not functions she has to learn to practice; these abilities are an innate
part of the feminine character. The healing touch is a natural
gift in every sister, nurse and mother. Not to hurt but to aid,
not to break apart but to put together are enviable qualities
in the female psyche that the male can never emulate. The
energies of man may adjust better to the ever-present hazards of smaller irritations, but in the great crises of life it is
the spiritual resilience of the woman that shapes the outcome of events. When the so-called hopeless situation appears and man is tempted to yield to defeat, the woman will

discover flickering signs of hope that can reverse the tragic circumstances.

During the historical drama of Calvary, women showed their strength in the charisma of compassionate love. At the same time that Christ was betrayed by an Apostle, condemned by a man in Roman armor, pierced in the heart by the lance of a soldier, women faithfully proclaimed the innocence of their beloved Redeemer. It was Pilate's wife who implored her husband, "Have nothing to do with that man; I have been upset all day by a dream I had about him" (Matt. 27:19). Totally oblivious of the mockery of the rabble, the pious women of Jerusalem showed their sorrow and love for the Lord. Whether driven by historical appointment or by their strong desire to show their sympathy, they consoled their Savior at the moment when He needed consolation the most. Until the bitter end, they never wavered as they stood beside the cross. And Christ, in remembrance of their faithfulness, appeared first to a woman after His resurrection. "And the women came up to him and, falling down before him, clasped his feet. Then Jesus said to them, 'Do not be afraid; go and tell my brothers that they must leave for Galilee; they will see me there' " (Matt. 28:9–10).

Women of today, in their understandable efforts to achieve a more dignified evaluation in the male-dominated structure of our society, may be tempted to channel their competitive energies into a direction that does not enhance their femininity. As they try to compensate for several long-established inequalities, they may jeopardize values that are basic elements in the character of womanhood. When following the simplistic logic of "if men can do it, so can we," women easily forget that in becoming equal they may surrender the prerogatives that make them attractive and superior to men. Equality is a far more elusive process than a purely mathematical equation. The condition of being equal is always achieved at a price; in gaining something, something else is lost. Why are women willing to give up so much when the gains are hardly worth the exchange? Total equality between the sexes would not only obliterate woman's capacity for human understanding, it would also remove from life the beautiful tensions created by the difference in the sexes. "To be at our best in order to impress" is needed to make life more exciting. How boring a world in which everyone is equal!

To rival man on masculine terms makes the woman unfeminine and neutral. As the flower is never really free if it is cut from its roots, so is a woman never really liberated when she ignores her own distinctive qualities. Only in the reverence and respect of each other can a just solution emerge from our many trials and errors. "Charm is deceitful, and beauty empty; the woman who is wise is the one to praise" (Prov. 31:30).

The very future of our civilization may well depend on the quality of values that the modern woman considers inviolable. If the woman, the source of life, protects life with all the powers under her command, life will flourish. If living becomes an expendable notion of relative value only, no other value will remain sacred. Some of the present predicaments have been caused by women themselves; other conditions have been forced upon them by circumstances over which they had little control. Whatever the causes of present tensions and strains in women, we cannot gloat over the defeated woman, because in *her* defeat we all are defeated. Without her faith, compassion, love and example, life itself is threatened by the male element of violence and destruction. If that is ever allowed to happen, no one, not even the wisest woman or man, will be able to predict what the future will hold.

Chapter 6

COMMUNITY

Kindness within a community
Excites the will to strive;
The dream is then enlightened
And in faith is kept alive.

From the beginning of time, history has shown that people driven by gregarious instincts prefer to live in some form of organized community instead of living alone. Age-old concerns for safety and desires to improve the quality of life impel them to seek friendship and the sharing of ideas. When clustered together they feel less vulnerable than those who are by themselves and unprotected. The security enjoyed by individuals joined in common interests and corresponding goals gives such an advantage that the occasional disadvantages of being close together diminish in importance. Prosperous living conditions are now within our reach because far-sighted men and women have pooled their spiritual and material resources for the common good. Present-day communities achieve a strength of maturity that justifies their heralded existence. Because of such spirited cooperation, neighborhood family groups, convents, retreat houses, organized clubs, condominium-style apartments and even small family relationships all have become an important part of our community mode of living.

  Communis—Together defines the essence of living in a group and clearly expresses the possibility of combining the "power of the many" for the "benefits of the one." Shared needs and anxieties become far less threatening than when faced alone. Families eagerly respond to the natural call of living close together, not only to safeguard the lives of their children but also to strengthen the security of the community. When cut off from the protective arm of a chosen group, people are more readily victimized by symptoms of fear and loneliness; when surrounded with companions, they absorb as though by osmosis the courage provided by united strength. How wise the scriptural warning, "Woe to the man alone!"

The advantages of being in close contact with others are practical and worthwhile if we are able to bear with the limitations. A willingness to adjust to the difference in personalities makes it easier for each to accommodate the other. By becoming conscious of our own imperfections and by not insisting upon our own way too often, we learn to be tolerant of our neighbor's shortcomings and to accept the other's ideas. If God is able to love us as we are, should we not be able to extend the same privilege to others?

Communities do not exist unless they are made to happen. Once established, organizations need to be reinforced continuously in order to prevent decay. As a living process, a society renews itself in meaning and vitality through the assistance and contributions of the members. The talent of the one becomes the bonding agent of the many. Responsible men and women, needed to create a bright and thoughtful whole, are far more important to any community than written rules and material fortune. The group founded on excellence will make fewer mistakes than the one without principles.

When we choose to join forces with a marriage partner, a society of people or a social organization, we obligate ourselves to support certain goals. To endorse an ideal without fighting for its cause is to enjoy the fruits without sharing the labor. The rise and fall of any marriage, neighborhood or society depends upon the industry and generosity of its members. Success is possible when duties are unselfishly performed; decline is probable when responsibilities are ignored. The inevitable breakups are often initiated by members who refuse to contribute time and understanding. Not to believe in each other, however quietly, may be equally as damaging as loud condemnations. When defeat is accepted without a battle for survival, a lack of courage and endurance is usually evident. Are we worthy of the *gift* of life if our *faith* in life is missing?

Promises are made to be kept. When the "I" expands into the communal "We," the obligations of living within a community become as serious as our most intimate personal concerns. The moment we link our fate with the fate of another person or group, our mental prowess and psychological resources cease to be purely private property. Prudence, discretion and wisdom enrich our personal fortunes and improve the quality of leadership required for the success of our group. Moral and spiritual values will be developed more by members who are born initiators and models of creativity than by impressive financial contributions. The ones who lose interest and disassociate themselves from agreements previously made reveal a weakness of integrity. For them to refuse the burdens of the association and yet enjoy the benefits forces others to compensate for the lost promises. "If our life in Christ means anything to you, if love can persuade at all, or the Spirit that we have in common, or any tenderness and sympathy, then be united in your convictions and united in your love, with a common purpose and a common mind" (Phil. 2:1–2).

Emotional preferences for a special type of community cannot be disregarded without the possibility of psychological harm. Since a spontaneous attraction toward a particular group of people can be more reliable than logical conclusions, the pull of the heart is often the safest signal to follow. The measure of our feelings stands next to the prompting of the mind. This does not mean that "likes and dislikes" are infallible directives; it means that it is possible for such feelings to result from providential responses. In our search for the values of life, many of us depend on the healthy intuitions chartered by experience.

Stressful attitudes that weaken the bonds of "together-ness" would be less serious if people involved were able to reveal the confrontation in dialogue. It is possible for ani-mosities, even those nurtured over long periods of time, to grow dim after a reasoning in conversation. A colloquy of-fered with patience removes the doubts that close living con-ditions are bound to foster. To hear someone say "I love you" makes the sun shine even at night. And if the parent and child, husband and wife, friend and friend would join together in open discussion instead of suffering in silence, the clouds of separation would eventually disappear from the horizon. Unfortunately, in our modern life-styles we seem to focus more attention on radio and television than on the person, a habit that continues to undermine so many of our personal relationships. Those of us never in a mood for an earnest conversation are in need of reviewing important priorities. This does not imply that every attempt to com-municate must be solemn or serious; occasionally light-hearted laughter is needed to defuse tensions.

Not all forms of dialogue are equally productive; often, words are spoken to parade fluency rather than substance. If truth is interpreted through slogans and if half-truths are used as acceptable means of expression, solutions remain clouded and unworkable. Knowledge serves us well only as long as it is employed in an authentic and honest manner. Oratory that seeks popularity at the price of accuracy deep-ens the roots of the conflict instead of promoting an agreea-ble settlement. Speakers who use clever phrases to hide real intentions not only betray their own integrity, they also frus-trate the listener who came to hear the truth. Camouflage is a crude deception of the divine gift of intelligence. Of what use is the best idea if it is sacrificed to arrogance and vanity?

Every community faces occasional moments of failure. Conflicts that arise from misunderstandings beyond the reach of human speech accumulate so much bitterness that con-versation by itself offers little satisfaction. Words not sup-ported by deeds lack the power to convince. People disillu-sioned with their chosen community have to be exposed to convincing actions before they can abandon their antagonistic postures. Overtures to redeem the cause of the bitterness invite the possibility of a lasting agreement. When a performance confirms love and affection, it is easier to forget the offensive words and remember only the love that said them.

The guilt connected with occasional failures can seldom be attributed to a single cause. Placing the full blame on the members who ignore their duties is an inadequate supposition. A major reason for the lack of accomplishment can be the indifferent and undisciplined mood of the entire group. When mass inertia is allowed to set in, when the trivial edges out the serious, a noncaring attitude is fostered in which ideas are frustrated. Even when there are members interested and eager to add their spiritual and mental capabilities, a dull antagonism can permeate the atmosphere and spread discouragement if an association is weak in cooperation. Can anyone be blamed for seeking intellectual stimulation elsewhere if the home front is sterile and unmanageable?

The concept that obligations toward a community are fulfilled simply because rules and regulations have been followed is misleading. Precepts and commands point to a general orientation, but they can never be so precise that initiative and freedom are abolished. The mechanical submission to rules without inner participation of mind and soul brings out the puppet, not the responsible human being. Decisive orders and actions are necessary indeed if the executive arm of any society or relationship is to exercise its powers and function with authority; it would be naïve, however, to think that such commands always embrace and delineate every detail of service. Rules can never be written to satisfy the total scope of human endeavors. To honor the needs of a chosen community is a basic principle of common living, but in this act of honoring, the whole subject, the "I," must be brought to maturity. If love is the dynamism of any dedication, obligations and legalities will assume their proper place. Even with the best of regulations, an absence of love hinders the establishment of a meaningful and harmonious interaction.

If a group of people working or living together is to be protected from the danger of "spinning inward" (self-preoccupation), dialogue must take first place. Heeding another one's advice sometimes provides the only shelter from the voice of ignorance. Relationships grow stronger when an honest conversation replaces intervals of isolation. Real problems are solved not by silence or hasty confrontations but by a constant exchange of relevant thoughts. Members who are sincerely interested and care about the ideals that unite them all confirm the fact that each one represents an effective voice in the total interchange of hope and trust. Opportunities for the contribution of the one enhance the growth of the whole, whereas the stifling of individual participation initiates an eventual decline.

Unfortunately, straightforward and patient explanations will not always offer the most conducive method of settling a dispute. Many of the predicaments that strain our human encounters need greater attention than the usual open and logical discussions. Although our ears, lips and curiosity may be receptive to the meaning of the speech, conflicts can lodge beyond the level of general understanding. An answer given is not always satisfactory if it fails to reach the deeper roots of the antagonistic state of affairs. A mysterious "more" is needed to lay bare the motivations that first induced strife into the atmosphere. This "more" will come only from the spiritual heritage into which we were born. When all other means of solving a dispute fail, the soul familiar with an eloquence the mind can never imagine has to come to our assistance.

Fortunately, the intervention of harmony relieves and calms the unpleasant situations that arise from dissent. Community members whose very presence inspire peace are a greater asset than intellectual giants or financial tycoons. Their patient reactions, stressing unity instead of dissension, insure that time is not wasted on needless feuds. Members surrounded with supportive companions become interested and more resourceful in their approach to challenging situations. As long as truth does not suffer in accepting the decision of the group, a harmony of opinions and interests should be a common goal. Obviously, the insight of one person is more prone to error than the experience and wisdom of several. Although peace at any price cannot be expected to offer long-lasting solutions, peace at the price of vanity should be considered.

Generally, people are not quarrelsome. The average person becomes ill at ease in the presence of those who are undecided and visibly upset. When circumstances present an option, very few will prefer "strife" to "tranquility and quiet." Individuals in conflict are not always playing the role of the spoiler; they may feel that a clash of opinions provides the rich potential for a more comprehensive grasp of the truth. Undoubtedly, an opposite viewpoint that remains stubborn and refuses to listen to another will lead into stagnant antagonism; it takes a meaningful divergence of ideas if a profitable dialogue is to result. Dissent for the sake of a more thorough view of the issue impels our logic to express its position in clear and decisive terms, avoiding ambiguities and dubious conclusions. A thesis is more impressive if it weathers not only the scrutiny of an agreeable audience but also the sharp critique of uncommitted and cautious observers.

In community dissension, if we try to heap the guilt onto others, it may be that we are irritated by the splinters we see in their eyes while we disregard the beam in our own. Evaluations that originate in selfishness and resentment seldom afford an unbiased and just appraisal. Anger easily blinds sight. How many of us are able to summon the inner strength needed to silence the voice of revenge? Only when communities strictly adhere to a code of impartial justice will all sides have a fair chance to meet in agreement. What is sowed will be harvested.

Legitimate disagreements interject something more into life than the arid formalism of purely intellectual conclusions. Without the challenge of opposition, life could well deteriorate into a logical game in which mechanical replies overshadow the real drama of life. Contradictions can bring out the best as well as the worst in us. Because words by their very presence can provoke either hostility or peace, it is possible for the stimulation of such contradictory discussions to result in progress for the community. To deny or ignore the presence of discontent could very well result in the loss of many of its benefits. Without new and creative impulses to augment the common pool of experience and wisdom, repetitious duties and programs could very easily deaden the spirit of even the most dedicated members.

Problems are rarely solved unless they are recognized and freely discussed. When friction is buried in silence or contempt, the discord lingers on, festering beneath the surface of artificial harmony as it awaits another chance to erupt. Any community that looks upon serious conflict as a threat to progress cuts itself off from possible sources of inspiration, which are needed to deepen insight and strengthen perception. Obviously not every sound of discontent can be silenced with sincere affection and good will because there are always a few members in every assembly who are not able to find the key to the heart of others. Perennially at war with themselves, they lose their sensitivities for peace. Not satisfied with the worth of their own personality, they vent their anger on the accomplishment of others. Their critical remarks offered under reasonable justification reveal inner conflicts not yet admitted or resolved. Living together with such resentful and irritable people in marriage, religious life or business arrangements requires the heavenly gift of patience. And some men and women do have this patience; they quietly deny their own satisfactions so that others can survive. These are the ones to be called "our saints."

As people vary, so do controversies; they appear in many shapes and forms, not all of them honest. Some patterns of contention use disguise as a favorite ploy. A quarrel that pretends to be inspired by common sense sometimes is caused by disturbed emotions. Many hurt feelings and ruffled sensitivities choose to parade under a cloak of rationality in order to secure sympathy from the unattached observer. Uncontrolled outbursts of jealousy reveal a lack of discipline camouflaged with pretense. A good performance is often criticized when the performer is disliked, and the glory of another's success is diminished when envy rules the mind. The moment that feelings alone circumscribe the area of the conflict, great reserve is needed before a just appraisal can be made. When both heart and mind erupt with equal vigor, wisdom is able to recognize the truth.

Delight and contentment are infectious. A community enthusiastically supported thrives on the eternal fountain of youth. Are there any limitations on the achievements of joy and satisfaction? Even burdens lose their weight when carried with happiness and pleasure. An encouraging and hopeful attitude can undo the damage inflicted by gloomy and cynical insinuations. Laughter and a show of love among partners or members is one of the greatest signs of success.

All communities, including individual families and large religious organizations, will gain from the healthy attitude of kindness. People who are sincerely convinced that pride and respect form a consensus of trust within the unit are valuable leaders. Occasionally, however, the self-respect within a particular group will become so exclusive that outsiders are treated as intruders. Regardless of how large a membership the community enjoys, it is still only a small part of the greater unit . . . the whole society of people. No one should ignore the fact that the needs of every individual must be taken into the final account. For one group to act as a privileged caste fighting for its own specific interests at the expense of the others indicates that mutual commitments and support have yielded to selfishness and greed. A group that has lost its public spirit and concern for the needy slips into decline even though outward appearances seem to be vigorous and strong. When individuals have to be reminded or coerced to be considerate, it is obvious that they are not open to the needs of the common cause. Although human nature in its very essence is generous and open-hearted, situations do arise which drain a person so completely that eventually nothing else matters except the recovery from daily exhaustion. In the small community of the family, parents and children can absorb one another's attention to such a degree that hardly any energy or strength is left to care for the anxieties of a friend or neighbor. At times, this is acceptable; it should however be considered the exception, not the rule.

Understandably, community living can be extremely difficult unless the privacy of each individual is respected. An occasional request to be "left alone" should always be honored, especially when a long-needed rest is in order. The priest or nun in a religious community, the tired partner in a marriage relationship, or the working aide in a nursing home obviously deserve a time of aloneness. As a consistent mode of action, however, this preference is not desirable because such a habit harms the psychological balance of the individual and also affects the quality of community life. When the spirit of helpfulness and the mutual respect for others become inactive, selfishness and isolation take over.

Wherever there are communities, there are meetings. Not only is Christ present when two or three gather in His name, problems are also present. So it was in the time of the Apostles and so it is now. The usefulness of these get-togethers depends on how well we listen, understand and love. Corporate officials who doubt the effectiveness of "groups in session" are probably concerned over the great number of meetings that should never have been held at all. Such gatherings are indeed a waste of time when members fail to appear on time, pretend to be indifferent or stray from the important issues. On the other hand, carefully organized discussions generally play a most sustaining role in the development of skills and attitudes. If the "why" is made clear, the "how" quickly generates growth.

Ultimately, we are always alone together. Our chosen community is not expected to be our final destiny or fulfillment. Even though associations of people play a valuable role in our search for eternal life, the group should never assume total responsibility for the spirituality of its members. We came from God alone, and alone we shall return. In our continuing quest for the Divine, our closest friends are only complementary. Although fidelity, loyalty and compassion are offerings we render to one another, personal crucial decisions will always rest within ourselves. The authority required for moral judgments and psychological decisions belongs to the individual, assisted when necessary by the group. Of course, conscience is not absolute and must listen to the Church, but a community that assumes unreasonable prerogatives surely infringes on our innate, God-given rights. The corporate heart has to respect the needs of the individual soul to grow on personal merit, so that in living with others, in the solitude of our search for God, we will be able to enjoy the enriching experience of friendship within a chosen community.

Chapter 7

LONELINESS

Loneliness is chosen,
A preference for the Me;
When one stands up in friendship
How lonely can one be?

When people gifted with intuitive insights probe the spiritual and mental health of a group, the majority of them conclude that loneliness is one of the most pervasive sufferings a person has to endure. The restless man and woman, confused as to who they are and where they belong, feel abandoned and graceless in a world drifting along without purpose and spiritual goal. Unable to relate to a motivation of honesty and truth, they consider inner values and convictions as luxuries pursued only by religious societies. Immersed in the ruthless battle of survival, good and evil are often submerged in the "know-how of life."

Professionals who deal with distress link loneliness to the current malaise of alcoholism, drug abuse and suicide. Young business executives, idealistic professors and modern homemakers who lose confidence and self-esteem seek solace in whatever will block out their apprehensions of reality. Some enjoy a drink for the sake of drinking and some drink to excess in order to forget; others depend on drugs to numb their minds or overcome inhibitions. Those who abuse liquor or drugs eventually find themselves so abandoned that life itself ceases to be a gift.

Loneliness, which is characterized by the inability to give, has its roots in so many human emotions that a common denominator can hardly be established. Because of physical or mental disabilities, emotionally immature individuals become prime candidates for voluntary withdrawal. Aware of being unequal to what is expected or required, they foster shy and regressive attitudes. The fear that their real or imaginary deficiencies will be put on view forces a pretense, and they look for corners in which to hide the real self. Their preference for loneliness grows even in a crowd of people because they are afraid that their inadequacies will be discovered. Only when the self-conscious person is unchallenged can the need to pretend be alleviated. As long as the weakness is not discovered, the individual is able to sustain a front of relative security. Although a strong personality may never be developed, certain joys can be garnered in peace through the power of pretending.

Feeling rejected on account of physical disabilities and personal limitations is not the same as the self-rejection built up on memories from a disgraceful past. When someone is determined never to lift the veil from previous shameful deeds, the creative strength available to enrich the wonders of life is lost in the preoccupation of hiding. Latent talents and keen reasoning powers are stymied by the mind absorbed with regrets over events of long ago. A deeply anchored sense of guilt can corrupt every effort to begin again. Unable to find a convincing answer to "Why did it happen to me?" the self-inflicted victim tries to exile the inner perturbation to an area less accessible to emotions. It is hoped that when the disruptive memory is tucked away from the mainstream of life, the misdeed will starve from lack of attention. Unfortunately, however, what is suppressed remains very much alive, ready to reappear at the most unexpected moment. Healing, perhaps through a humble confession, is the only way for a sad and mournful past to replace itself with acceptance, understanding and future joy.

Meaningful relationships are next to impossible as long as inner conflicts are allowed to fester. Wounded pride incarcerates the hungry soul. Punishing ourselves for past transgressions forces us to center so much attention on the self that there is nothing left to invest in our friends. If the voice that accuses also obliterates a voice that forgives, it is not able to respond with compassion. Concentration on a personal song of lamentations diffuses the sensitivities needed to understand the sadness of others. And when suspicions and incriminations mingle freely and direct our thoughts, we make little time available for our loved ones in need. Only a conscience in harmony with divine authority and at peace with self has the capacity to listen and respond with clarity. Can we expect others to open their doors of understanding if our own doors are tightly closed?

Being well adjusted to both past and present does not make a person invulnerable to "surprises." Powers beyond our volition, happenings independent of expediencies often confront us with uncontrollable situations forcing us to acknowledge that a real Master shapes our destiny. Decisions affecting the future of our existence are not always our own prerogatives; incidents can happen that annul our fondest dreams and aspirations. Afflictions considered in the divine analysis as a momentary sorrow can become for some of us the "tragedy of a lifetime."

Responses given in times of crisis differ according to faith, life-style and education. Certain types of people grow audacious in the fury of a storm and insist on fighting their way to the saving shores. Their energies revive immediately when the shattered life is viewed as a challenging invitation to rebuild. Others, discouraged with defeat, are swept away by the wave of disaster and tend to surrender helplessly from the blow of fate.

Since even the most traumatic experiences are subject to our freedoms, we need never remain captives of distress. It is within our power to determine the final effects that a situation will have on our life. "Good" and "bad" depend so much on our inner point of reference. There is always the opportunity to appraise misery as a way of measuring our resilience to survive and conquer. If we know how to turn a tragedy into a mysterious source of strength, a calamity can be a boon to inner fortune. Losses can result in gains. Only when adversities are permitted to diminish our vitality do we face disappointment or loneliness. On the other hand, the ability to transform sadness and defeat into joy and triumph needs tremendous faith in the God who knows why light is mingled with darkness. Without such a belief, the transformation will not be accomplished.

Although a burden shared is a burden lightened, at times it seems part of our destiny to confront distress and desolation by ourselves. Even after Christ begged His Apostles to stay awake and pray with Him, He found himself alone. Loneliness, not His choice nor ours, is an occasional necessity imposed upon us without our consent. And in the midst of such turmoil, when we are without a companion, what else can we do but marshal our strength and pray? Are we of so little faith that we cannot cry out to God during a time of tragic misfortune? When one implores divine help, a special assistance of grace is experienced. Many, many people in near despair have discovered the unexpected drive of divine origin. Is it any wonder that so many of us begin to pray when a sudden crisis exhausts our lines of supply? By reaching out to God in our moments of abandonment, we make ourselves open to His support even though we are not always aware of His presence.

In His divine munificence God bestows gifts upon us far beyond our keenest expectations. There may be times, however, for reasons not always clear to us, when He deems it fitting to take away the things or people we most enjoy. The death of a loved one, the end of a friendship or the loss of hard-earned benefits create a void not easily filled again. Joys shared intensify in beauty; when experienced alone they can be sad reminders of happier days gone by. Although memories are gladly cherished, contemplations of the past never make up for the real. For some, the long-ago gift of love becomes the greatest sorrow. Occasionally, a person crushed by the terrible blow of losing something special may see death as a welcome relief. With sadness as the only thing left, each new day repeats the lonely pains of separation and the unanswerable question of *why*.

But in spite of losses, the streams of existence have to keep flowing so that in the flow our lives will deepen, spread out and clarify. Even if the joys taken away appear irreplaceable, life imposes upon us the sacred obligation to give ourselves another opportunity to begin again. The glory of God reveals itself most convincingly in being fully *alive*. Growth must never be allowed to come to a standstill. New initiatives, new choices have to be discovered and other friendships developed in order to fill the painful emptiness. A different phase in life is ready to commence, less fulfilling perhaps but with enough challenge to make us want to start anew. The seeds of new growth are a reminder that future hopes remain the one force which should never face defeat. The gift of survival cannot be wasted. The greater the loss, the more pressing our duty to reject loneliness and revive the determination to prevail. The world can indeed be ours again if we are forceful enough to claim it; only the collapse of the human will, which is despair, or the revolt of the human will, which is pride, can prevent us from trying again. To give up on ourselves and others is one of the more unfortunate prerogatives of human freedom. We are at liberty to resurrect our dreams as much as we are free to direct our own demise. Since God does not force the hand of our will, our actions continue to be our own responsibility.

The best time to stop the growth of loneliness is in the beginning. The longer we wait, the more difficult the effort to break through the wall of isolation. Selfishness or pride makes our personality less attractive than we realize. Even when not expressed, the feeling of considering ourselves better than others reveals itself and makes people cautious in their approach. If we are slow to listen because we presume to have all the answers, what chances are there for a successful dialogue? Whenever our affections remain unrequited, when loved ones diminish in number and the knocking at our door becomes less frequent, it is time to discover what is wrong. It may well be that our own attitudes will be found at the root of the alienation!

Popular opinion targets the frail and elderly as the primary sufferers of loneliness and isolation. The thinking is that because of impairments in sight and hearing, the older generation finds it difficult to establish bonds of new encounters. Contrary to that belief, however, research data conclude that it is the adolescents and young adults who are the most lonely. Our youth, desperately searching for identity, find it extremely difficult to interact and relate to anyone outside of their group. Many of them, reared in broken families, have never experienced the warmth and security provided by the tightly knit home unit. Bitterness can play an overpowering role when young people discover that they have been abandoned by a parent. Disenchantment sets in when they realize that the values taught are not the values lived. Disillusioned by moral codes that are established but seldom put into action, they are prompted to follow their own ethical norms with casual justification. One hypocrisy is threatened with another, resulting in our present moral confusion.

Strange as it may seem, many young people are sensitive to rejection; in their attempt to avoid such a reaction, they call upon parents and friends to approve the "modern" way of living. Nonapproval or enforced objections cause experimenting youth to flee into greater loneliness. Their way has to triumph if there is to be any way at all. Is it any wonder that the number of young men and women who take their own lives is on the increase? When they sever their connection with their past and see no "ideal" in their future, the present moment seems meaningless and absurd.

Obstacles arise in life not to be obeyed but to be overcome. A poor start in life, although regrettable, is not the finalizing element in the development of human existence. The majority of people who achieve greatness had a very modest start in life. Difficulties accepted with integrity and faith bring the best of a character to the surface. Adversities do not shape the character; they only reveal the character that the person had before the misfortune took over.

Precarious as the times are, the outlook is surely not beyond redemption. Our youth, always considered the noble hope for a better future, can turn many a deficiency into a promising asset. However lonely individual prospects may appear, the world always is filled with excitement, adventure and stunning triumphs; only when our younger generation realizes what the future could hold will they focus their attention and talents on promising beginnings rather than on premature endings. To rejoin the mainstream of life may be difficult for them at first, but their consistent endeavors to reach out will bring personal rewards. In this process of reconciliation, many of the elderly will be found friendly, not antagonistic. There is little chance for survival when people are alone and separate, but by working together, the building of a future harmonious to all can be within the realm of probability.

Loneliness is not to be confused with solitude; loneliness points to unresolved inner conflicts, and solitude points to disciplined strength. To be alone is not the same as being lonely. Occasionally all of us need to find a private space where things we do not understand can be sorted out. Our right to privacy is not a privilege but a glaring necessity, especially if we hope to keep our mind healthy in a world of contradictions. The pressing urge to separate ourselves from others does not always indicate selfishness or lack of concern. For the giving person, solitude is the quiet state that makes available a welcome respite from the incessant demands made on time and talent. Away from others, each one discovers the resilience needed to guide and inspire.

"Togetherness" and "aloneness" are not competitors; they are complementary forces that sustain each other's vitality and zest. In the restless whirl of activity, it is easy to lose the preeminent characteristics that make up our personality. We need to reinforce the true self with the quietude of stiller moments. A faithfulness to individuality is renewed when different aspects of our daily existence converge into one. It is a mistake to conclude that we help our friends only by talking together. Certainly at times the spoken word must be heard to alleviate the pressures of loneliness, but it is unreasonable to expect that anxieties must be addressed through speech alone. There are many emotional disturbances that respond to a physical presence without being probed through speech. The ability to sympathize and relate to one another makes a greater contribution to healing than the fluency of speech. When little is said, so much can be understood.

For married people, solitude is the most useful way to prevent nearness from turning into boredom. A time to rest, to plan and to think without interruption improves concentration and restores freedom of thought. Inevitable personal limitations lose their cutting edge when the healing is nurtured within the self. It is easier to absorb the pressures of anger when a person is alone, in full power of self-preservation; irritations given a chance to mellow usually stop hurting. In the end, the gentleness of spirit recalls not what was said but the love that said it.

When the shadows of loneliness are allowed to outgrow reason, they can reach an intensity beyond control and become a veritable threat to life itself. People who suffer without consolation are easily tempted to give up. Is there any burden as heavy as the one which is carried alone? Suicidal tendencies are on the increase, but unless we contribute our share toward changing this very human problem, we cannot stand in judgment. Only the powers of the heart are strong enough to resurrect the ambition to live. Being loved fortifies the courage and confidence to face hardships and trouble. When the very being of another person becomes part of ourselves, we use the other's strength to confront our own perplexities. Ultimately, the sharing of self with a finite being reveals the nearness of an infinite Being. The powers from beyond channeled through the human heart are more fortifying than any effort conceived by man or woman.

With its own dynamic and irrepressible vitality, love tends to serve not only as a transient pleasure but as the most creative force the soul shall ever experience. Life itself is sometimes sacrificed before love is betrayed. How true the saying that a thing is perfect when it fulfills the purpose for which it was created. Two people in love with each other experience a miracle not visible to anyone else. Real love stirs in us the knowledge that we are much more than we think we are, whereas love feigned makes us aware of what we are not. To abandon the person once loved raises the question of whether love was there in the beginning. True love seldom has the chance to grow when the outburst of passion is triggered by aroused emotions, infatuations or lust. The emotions of love shown to others simply because we need them become a means of satisfying our selfish desires. What could have been a most beautiful challenge in life ends in a legendary tale of selfishness and pride. Man and woman were created to master the most human challenge of life which is *love;* if this summons is failed, then life itself has failed. "As long as we love one another God will live in us and his love will be complete in us" (1 John 4:12).

Raising our national symbol on the arid space of a conquered moon was an illustrious performance of which our nation is justly proud. Less dramatic but equally as important is the raising of new hope in a lonely soul. Can anything compare with the rescue of a human being who suffers the agony of being forsaken? The promise of a friend, "I am here with you, whatever comes," opens up courage on earth and renewed respect in heaven. Resurrecting confidence and trust is the true gift of friendship.

The final chapter on loneliness will never be written by human imagination alone. The unseen hand of God who gave His life on the cross adds the unknown dimension to the sufferings of total abandonment. When viewed purely from the human standpoint, the state of being lonely is often considered distasteful and sad. From God's point of view, however, loneliness is not time wasted but time invested in eternity. Through the grace that Christ earned for us, we are empowered to transform the visible darkness of loneliness into the invisible light of faith and hope. The experience of being forsaken carries within itself the promise of its own glorious fulfillment. If we can accept our moments of helplessness as a visitation of the Lord, as a reminder of our exile from God, loneliness will be the final cleansing that readies us for the divine embrace.

Chapter 8

MY DAY

Fill my days with meaning, Lord,
Make spare my tears and pain;
Touch the hearts of those I love
That none may live in vain.

"How was your day?" is a characteristic query that offers either pure civility or serious concern. Most of us find it comparatively easy to cope with questions that do not invade the privacy of our character or the quality of our lifestyle. A casual inquiry is matched with light-hearted banter; when politeness asks, courtesy answers. To elaborate would be unnecessary. If we surmise from the tone of voice, however, that sincerity, not curiosity, is at the root of the discussion, we quickly adjust to a deeper, honest reply. Real solicitude deserves to hear of the experiences that have brought us joy and sadness.

What is the significance of a day? Do we attach any meaning to the passing hours or do we see them only as a time-substance without any allegiance to morality and valor? Can a day be a challenge, or is it little more than a period of monotony and boredom?

Those of us receptive to the inspiring values of our world accept a day as a gracious earthly commodity, an object of heavenly concern in which both heaven and earth are shareholders. As our partner, silent or otherwise, God is interested in the quality of our performance and expects a return from His investment. We are in need of Him just as He is in need of us. The way we treat a day is recorded in our own memories and also in the mind of the Divine. As a friend, our day is a firm advocate; as an enemy, it is strong enough to destroy us. Time is of such importance to some people that they would gladly spend a fortune to buy back one day of their lives!

Our days are never neutral; either they transform us or we transform them. When we fail to impose our will, the day assumes the right to determine its own course. Without the courage to rule, we will be ruled. Good and evil do not lodge in the various happenings of the day; good and evil are characteristics deeply embedded in the heart. A day is deemed happy or sad not on account of what has happened but because of the response we gave to what happened. What we make of it, makes us. That which one person will curse another will learn to accept and sanctify. "Those who went sowing in tears now sing as they reap" (Ps. 126:5).

Success is a life-creating energizer that instills in us the excitement and interest of moving forward. Days of achievement are marked with golden ink in our diaries and joyful thoughts in our memories. Such a day outshines the splendor of our day of birth. Island after island, mountain after mountain fall prey to the valor of the daring adventurers. Conscious of their discipline and power, they project their talents without rest in the attempt to make the last "possible impossibility" a reality. The look of weariness changes to triumph when victory shows its gracious wings and nests above the heavy ruins of defeat.

It is never wrong to celebrate a good day or to feel comfortable with earned applause. By making the most of opportunities and earning the respect and admiration of others, we acknowledge our duty to multiply our God-given talents. Does not every day beg us to take advantage of the chances to "make something of ourselves"? A day wasted here on earth limits our prospects for the world yet to come. Natural abilities that enrich life need to be exposed so that their presence can be appreciated. Being courageous enough to stand in control and face whatever risks appear can make a big difference in a person's life. It may be easier to trod the beaten path but that will never clear the way to light!

To work for success is a duty; not to depend upon success is wisdom. When we labor for the sole purpose of winning approval, seeking glory for the sake of glory, then all of our work is in vain. Greatness is being equally at ease with the joy of victory as with the taste of defeat. Those interiorly free, who toil whether applauded or rejected, attest to excellence and are the best candidates to win the race of humanity.

How wonderful it would be to have the choice of composing our own story of life! Surely our secret desires for fame could be obliged and the days of pain and suffering omitted. Ardently we could fashion ourselves as glamorous performers in an impressive tale of triumphs, with one day of bliss followed by continuing days of rapture. Lamentations and failures would not be allowed on the scene.

Reality, however, tells us that there are two hills on the ground we walk: Tabor and Calvary. Tabor was chosen by Christ for His resplendent transfiguration; Calvary became the place of His suffering and death. On various occasions, both these heights rise before our very eyes to wait for a response. How many of us have ever said *yes* to a day of bitterness and grief? How often have we freed our shoulders for the weight of the cross?

There are depths in the heart that are never revealed until pain and sorrow force them into maturity. People who have never experienced serious problems remain childish with an almost visible immaturity. This does not deny that failures and despair are capable of destroying the spirit and disrupting the harmony of mind; it simply points out that many of us would never discover the deeper insights of our character without a cleansing by the fires of hardship and tribulation. A period of suffering is not always necessary to enter the kingdom of heaven, but humble submission is expected if God in His all-embracing love decrees that a soul is to be saved through anguish. Only the tragic rebellion of the mind or the sad collapse of faith will keep distress from making a life more meaningful.

The cross of Calvary is blessed, not because it is a cross but because Christ carried it. Suffering is not welcomed for its own sake; it is accepted as a means to achieve a higher purpose. The knowledge that the Christ who suffered is our inspiration and companion makes possible our climb to the top of the hill. Regardless of how wretched a day seems to be, our life as a whole is in the hands of a trustworthy God. Those who lose touch with these beliefs are left to walk in darkness. "Yes, the troubles which are soon over, though they weigh little, train us for the carrying of a weight of eternal glory which is out of all proportion to them" (2 Cor. 4:17).

In the course of one day, success and failure can be reversible factors. Because neither is endowed with the characteristics of permanence, each can assume the shape of the other. Glorious beginnings have terminated in defeat and initial fears were crowned with remarkable success. Equanimity, that evenness of soul, enables us to cope with instabilities without becoming unstable ourselves. The ability to remain calm in surroundings that change from one extreme to another can be the natural effect of an unruffled temperament, or it can be a sign of the powerful grace of God. How wise the spiritual counselor who advises us not to become elated in times of exultation nor disheartened in periods of desolation. To recognize the changing elements in our daily experiences without being too deeply affected by the consequences attests to self-possession and a disciplined acceptance of God's will.

Reacting to uncertainties is not the same as responding to them. In a show of reaction, we allow aroused emotions to determine the future course of events; in a response, we appraise a situation according to perceptions of our mind. Reactions occur spontaneously, almost automatically, whereas a response is carefully filtered through the mind before it is put into words. Although neither is infallible, a greater chance for accuracy rests in a response. Usually, clearance by the mind is more reliable than guidance based upon fickle emotions.

Ordinary days do not exist because every day is special. Whatever we do in the name of the Lord results in a unique and irreplaceable performance. Human actions are identified by temporal views; they also participate in the redemptive plan of reconciliation and peace. The remark of Jesus, "What you have done to the least of my brethren, you have also done to me," refers to our deeds on earth and their eternal echoes in heaven. Our Savior's divine interest in our worldly investments confirms His great love for us. Just as God exacted tributes from the Israelites, He anticipates a contribution from each one of us. It does not matter how unglamorous or unnoticed our efforts may be. When it is inspired by the divine gift of love, a small act far surpasses the most pretentious deed.

Occasionally, at the end of a day, evening hours are filled with doubts instead of contentment and security. Since monotony and boredom demand more energy than we need for interesting accomplishments, fatigue or exhaustion does not imply success. Will our achievements really have a dynamic impact on the outcome of eternal destiny? Can our deeds bear the scrutiny of an impartial divine Judge? Were our decisions honest and worthy of His acceptance, or did they result from simple nervous energy? This can be one of the most important times of our day, and perhaps one of the most rewarding. "He will repay each one as his works deserve" (Rom. 2:6).

Time is most forcefully expressed in the shape of the present moment. Opportunities at hand are challenges we should never forfeit. Existence is measured by the day, not by years, months or seasons. If we focus on the happenings gone by or on the uncertainties of the future, will there be any energy left to dedicate ourselves to the present? Because of inertia or lack of spiritual readiness, some of us are never prepared to accept the tasks we face. Occasions full of promise are further sabotaged by an instinctive reluctance to "pay the price" of living in the *now*. A physical and mental alertness is conditioned by discipline and self-denial that some find too taxing for comfort. They prefer the detours of past memories or journeys into future dreams. "What no longer exists" or "what is yet to be" speaks with a less demanding voice than the immediate today. Divine providence opens up a variety of favorable paths; however, many people prefer the road to spurious escapades. Daydreams and nostalgia are chosen over commitment. The willingness to rise with the sun and accept responsibilities may be virtues of the past, but they are the attitudes needed if we hope to reap fulfillment.

A day not examined leaves a blank in the account of our daily achievements. When decisions of importance are left to pure chance, we invite the element of instability to jeopardize the consistency and order of our lives. A lack of interest in what the next day will bring leaves us unprepared for all the eventualities. Although life does not have to be a continuous laboring, well-ordered patterns of serious preparations can make the difference between success and failure. Confirming the prospects and workability of our inspirations does not make our endeavors failure-proof; being careful simply lessens the feelings of guilt if we fail.

Every day presents itself with a temperament we are not always able to predict. The span from morning to evening may radiate joy and relaxation or it may present its own style of melancholy. One day will bring a fruitful harvest of the seeds planted and another day will find the same strenuous efforts falling upon stony ground. Things we do not expect sometimes come forward, and what we do expect very often stays far behind. To keep pace with the uncertainties and surprises of daily living we have to learn to adjust and to accommodate.

Accommodation, unlike imitation, is a sign of courage and vitality. When we feel secure with our own established personalities, it will not be difficult to adapt our moods to the priorities of others. A decision to accommodate does not mean that we are giving "up" anything; rather it is a giving "in" to the more pressing needs of another. Accommodation rests on the resolve to help whereas imitation acts only to please. The divine Creator has assigned to each of us a one-of-a-kind character and individuality; a desire to imitate others, using them as models for inner development, ruins God's magnificent plan. The spirit of freedom knows how to adapt; the spirit of emptiness begs for support. A day proceeding on its own prerogatives and rhythm finds the mature person well adjusted to unforeseen eventualities; the weakling, however, will be frightened by things long before they happen.

Besides psychological maturity, we also need the support of religious inspiration in order to cope with the various dimensions of our daily strains. Human intellect of either the simple or the illustrious mind does not adequately relate to our spiritual hungers. It takes the meaning of the Sermon on the Mount to dispel spiritual or mental darkness. How difficult it is to persuade some of our learned men and women that there is an intelligence in faith far superior to their own! Deep religious convictions resurrect in our being the confidence needed to contend with present cynicism. Although trust in our divine Redeemer does not wipe away the sorrow from our days, it will direct us to a source of enlightenment and hope. "Raise me up when I am most afraid, I put my trust in you; in God, whose word I praise, in God I put my trust, fearing nothing, what can men do to me?" (Ps. 56:3–4).

Procrastination is another way in which we waste God's valuable gift of time. It is one of our less-engaging attributes, a common weakness that results in delay and diminishes our chances for successful achievement. Many disappointments have their origins in the postponement made necessary by our procrastinating behavior. By putting off until later a chore we should have completed immediately, we cut short present opportunities and perhaps others in the future as well. To expect that responsibilities will disappear when they are ignored favors inertia, not success. The best approach to a given problem is the actual solution. Working to realize a dream is the most efficient way to progress and the most effective manner of forming a courageous personality. If we keep abreast of the swing of the pendulum, we are already at work as the hour is striking!

One day of the week, the day of the Lord, urges us to activities of a different kind. Instead of our usual haste, anxiety and labor, this sacred day invites us to tranquility and peace. As every motion arises from rest and every harvest begins with a dying seed, so also must strong actions be rooted in calm and quiet. A heart functions better when it has a day of its very own. Recollections earned through activities yearn to be interrupted by serious labor; one without the other calls for its own demise. Too much excitement is tiring; too many memories defy their purpose. The monks of old who wrote on their bleak walls *ora et labora*—pray and work—must have discovered the need to be busy as well as the need to rest.

The day of the Lord was not planned to be spent in idleness; hours of meditation are highly productive. In prayer, dried out channels of love and communication are refilled with energy and perspectives, a replenishment not possible with pure activism. With dedication and determination, spirituality and contemplation can enhance an age of science, technology, psychoanalysis and biofeedback. Insights gained in prayer can provide an environment in which we come to understand and to judge the very purpose of existence. Our roots clamor for experiences that take us beyond the daily confrontations of materialism. The more we surrender to the ultimate hunger for truth, meaning and love, the more fully we respond to the call of creation. If the day of the Lord unites the sparkle of mind to the love in our hearts, then the seventh day is not only a day of rest, it is also a day of joyful fulfillment.

Every day offers opportunities that each one of us interprets with different intentions. Those who are attentive to private interests alone use the hours to expand the range of their influence and reputation. In their opinion, any attention invested with outsiders is a waste of time. A great number of people, more genial in nature, look forward to the many hours of the day as an occasion to encourage friends in their search for meaning. The worried mother watching at the bedside of her dying infant does not consider the day rewarding unless it is spent to comfort her child. The good doctor refuses to leave the wounded and the sick until he is able to relieve their pains. The priest does not call a day his own so long as his flock waits for encouragement and begs his forgiveness. Some people take a day for themselves; some live a day for others. Those who give are usually the happiest people in the world.

Particular memories stir deep regrets and many are the days we wish had never happened. Often have we abused God's precious gift of time, using it for purposes less than honorable. Perhaps we abandoned a lost soul who looked to us for friendship, or there may have been a time when we defied our own conscience by choosing the road that led to sin and betrayal! A few of our actions obviously were immature because we did not recognize the gift we wasted, but in many of them we were surely aware of the evil involved! How fortunate for us that regardless of the *why* or the *how*, we can always find that wonderful day which offers us a healing forgiveness. "God, create a clean heart in me, put into me a new and constant spirit, do not banish me from your presence, do not deprive me of your holy spirit" (Ps. 51:10–11).

A journey terminates when its intentions are accomplished. Eventually, our calendar will reach the one day without sequel, the day of our final hour. Our life, quite an uncertain enterprise, is constantly exposed to an abrupt ending. We never know in advance whether or not the morning, noon or evening will be our last. Death prefers not to announce its arrival. Acting as a master with a timing of its own, it carries out its mission without any concern for protests or requests for delay. Only for Christ has death made the one, unique allowance in order that the resurrection could take its place in history.

Although most of us prefer not to think of it, our date with death is approaching, and now is the time to prepare for it. Planning ahead relieves the element of surprise suffered by those who refuse to think of what is yet to be. Experiencing the presence of God within us and acknowledging our trust in His goodness helps us to face death with the anticipation of eternal life. Death will never come like a thief in the night if we look forward to welcoming it as a friend.

The last day on earth is a time for harvest. It was for Christ and so it will be for us. *Consummatum est . . .* it is consummated . . . as on that strange and gruesome afternoon of long ago when the pointers of time rested at three, when ominous clouds dazzled the curiosity of the crowd. The brilliant sun, always punctual in its arrival and departure, gave way to utter darkness. Vague terror took possession not only of the earth and rocks but also of the minds of the people who fled into silence as they realized their share of guilt in the death of their Redeemer. On this day, with His mission completed, Christ went home to His heavenly Father.

Our last day on earth, less dramatic to be sure, will be a summary of achievements and failures of our mission in life. Each of our days, with their highlights and disappointments, will be exposed to the unbiased glance of death. What will accompany us into eternity and what will go into the wasteland of the world will be clearly known by this mysterious figure. Each one of our days will move into the illuminating focus of our last day so that the merits and demerits of our deeds can be counted. Life for us will be over; our song will have reached its final melody, and our Lord will speak. At this, the most important moment of all, perhaps He will tell us what we want to hear: that we are saved by His inexhaustible mercy, saved by His infinite care. Then, and only then, will this last day on earth lead triumphantly to the arrival of the endless day in heaven.

Chapter 9

FEAR

Fear need not be our master,
Its counsel tends the mind;
By reaching beyond the failure
We leave our fears behind.

Fear, man's perennial companion, never waits for an invitation to cross the threshold of life. Welcomed or not, it invades the most secret corner of feelings and emotions without any concern for the suffering and pain of the victim. Even when fear starts a world-wide conflict, its fury is seldom abated or its force mitigated. Success in the strategy and manner of execution excites fear to pursue its prey until conquered. Although people who dwell in optimism usually put up a formidable resistance to the attack of fear, many of them surrender in the end.

In the past, anxieties were viewed as a reminder of the frailty of the human condition; now common fears have become a way of life. Many a situation that in the past was considered a simple annoyance is turned by our times into a most virulent menace. Suspicions and doubt take up residence in the very core of our being as an unmistakable presence that cripples the innocence and beauty of many a deed. No longer a transient boarder, apprehension emerges as a proprietor of the soul.

Preoccupation with fear has diluted tranquility of mind at all levels of existence—private, public, political and social.

Like a tidal wave, it rolls over sectors of civilization never before exposed to such dangers. Since nothing appears sacred or noble enough to escape the threat or assault of violence, the concept of security and protection remains constant in the mind of every individual.

Feelings of terror and dismay can trace their origins to the inner turmoils or outer unrest over which we have little control. A diffident attitude toward our abilities as well as concern over our turbulent mode of living provides the furrow for seeds of fright to grow. Whether the hostile emotion pesters us from within or without matters very little to the growth of panic. Once born, fear intensifies in its own right. Unless such painful feelings are arrested before the scarring begins, victims will die many times before they are buried.

Confidence is often shattered by worries that are unreasonable and without foundation. Imagination, ingenious but unreliable, can darken the mood so effectively that the message of new hope will never reach the portals of the soul. When the whole world is shrouded in gloom, what chance of survival is given to a cheerful thought? The feeling that "everything is lost" invites the thought of death as the only welcome relief.

The propensity to overbalance evil and emphasize adversity changes every thought of happiness into a sad and troubled ghost. Many of our daily encounters can be frightening indeed, and some of our feelings are surely justified; it is unfair, however, to concentrate on fear and disregard the numerous signs of love and consideration that still surround us. To allow a single experience to shadow our whole outlook on life fosters suspicions incompatible with "genuine relationships." Does the person, once betrayed, have the right never to trust again? Should the one who has been deceived by a lie hear a lie in every word? Promising aspects for a better future are poisoned if we let too many of our present moments be mutilated by fear. The world hides its best from those who brood over the worst!

A mentality steeped in hopelessness is not redeemed by logical arguments alone. Reason and intelligence are seldom effective enough to unmask emotions that have suffered from deception. Indirectly, it is love and patience, not rational considerations, that will restore a greater calm to the troubled heart. The person who cares is bound to offer more relief than the person who argues.

Often hostile in nature, fear serves also as a prudent counselor. A frightening experience can leave such a deep impression on our mind and emotions that chances for similar happenings are carefully avoided. For example, the revolting aftermath of sin may stir in us the resolve to avoid subsequent temptations; the person burned will shy away from fire. When truly convinced of the dangers of drugs, potential users will think twice before yielding to the pusher. Even in our schools, the traditional role of discipline has to be reemphasized and strengthened if we hope to teach respect and increase a regard for the law. Educators who insist on strong discipline in the classroom provide our youth with the source of courage needed to resist mischievous impulses. Any rule of life that allows young people to have all the things their instincts demand robs them of the desire to excel.

Thoughts we entertain shape the style of life we choose. What we think, we can become. Fears are as big or as small as our mind makes them. The depth and the clarity of our thoughts throw light on the elements that make up our character. By judging ourselves as incompetent we force the many challenges of life to remain unanswered. When we believe in ourselves, however, and develop our talents fully, we can wrestle away from life the many wonders it holds in its magical heart. It is the individual's responsibility to choose between the role of the hapless victim or the joyful heir to life. Those who walk in the dusk, afraid of the shadow, encounter shadows even when the sun is shining. To be destroyed by fear is a most humiliating epitaph on the tombstone of mental ambition. "In all you do be the master, and do not spoil the honor that is rightly yours" (Eccles. 33:23).

Ignorance is another factor that causes apprehensions to grow out of control. The torment of the unknown diminishes our satisfaction of the known. When science and technology surprise us with discoveries beyond comprehension, it is natural to become frightened with the thought of what will happen if the tide turns against us. No longer the innocent bystander, we have become the worried participant entitled to an exact accounting. Decisions that greatly affect the question of life or death, sickness or health should not be left exclusively to people in power. The news of mysterious weapons, widely heralded as being potent enough to eliminate life on our planet, spreads a variety of concerns among those of us who are eager to work for survival. Progress, which is a noble testimony to the human mind, bestows immeasurable benefits on mankind when it acts the role of the servant. The moment it is permitted to assume the prerogative of the master, however, progress can inflict irreparable damage on the vitality of the spirit. Substituting individual knowledge with a computer printout limits the range of creativity in human thought. Men and women formed to God's likeness resist all efforts intended to reduce them to the level of a tool. Discoveries must continue to be subject to our scrutiny before they are allowed to direct our lives.

Ignorance is not the same as error. Mental oversight or mistaken identities lead us to conclusions that do not always correspond to facts. Unfortunately, our judgments of people or things do not necessarily match reality; nor are pictures of a given situation that appear in our mind always substantiated by actual experience. While the "ignorant" lack knowledge, the "erroneous" misinterpret it.

Errors are induced by our own thinking or by extraneous sources of false information. If through default or delusion our actions or reactions are interpreted incorrectly, we have only ourselves to blame. A more careful analysis, perhaps, or a deeper understanding of the cause and effect could have produced a more truthful appraisal. Haste in coming to a wrong evaluation is often the preponderate reason why we say and do things that are offensive to truth. When other people are at the root of an emerging problem, it is easier for us to assume a sympathetic posture. Generosity flows more freely if the self is less involved with blame.

A self-righteous person who refuses to admit ignorance or acknowledge error can appear outwardly dictatorial and still be inwardly confused and suspicious. Individuals who strenuously cleave to narrow-minded interpretations feel threatened with contradictory ideas and beliefs, especially when prejudices are at stake. Convictions of their own infallibility are tested when other insights and opinions cast doubt over the correctness of their preconceived conclusions. A biased viewpoint does not do justice to truth, it merely confirms the insufficiency of a limited outlook on reality. If we filter judgments and appraisals of other people through the channels of our own intellectual intolerance, our perceptions of the world remain inaccurate and restricted. An occasional dip into self-righteousness will cause little harm, but when truth is at stake, personal attitudes have to submit to scrutiny. A false world never manifests the full intensity and beauty of the Divine.

Another vast gulf of frightened demons is opened up by physical fatigue or mental exhaustion. With our flesh censured by pain and weaknesses, fear ingratiates itself to a greater degree than when we are in the state of perfect health. Even the soul unbidden will fall prey to misgivings and apprehensions whenever energies are lagging. A body without strength precipitates defenselessness that, in turn, accelerates doubt and suspicions to sway our mind. Rare is the individual who refuses to let physical debilities infringe on the supremacy of mind. "My lament is still rebellious, that heavy hand of his drags groans from me. If only I knew how to reach him, or how to travel to his dwelling!" (Job 23:1–2).

Fears grow in strength when they are suppressed; worries intensify when they are restricted and ignored. At first, the appearance of excessive shyness, servile conformity and unnecessary cautions impress us as being prudent qualities of a humble personality. In retrospect, however, it may appear that such guileless behavior could be influenced, if not caused, by a timidity not admitted or recognized. Fears revealed can be resisted whereas fears held incognito enjoy free reign to grow and deepen. Pretending to be free of fear while inwardly we tremble creates a sense of false security. A puzzle to others, we now become an enigma to ourselves. Tribulations yield to healing only when their presence is acknowledged.

Fears do not decrease in energy when they expand their powers over nations or empires. Mass hysteria has recorded some of the ghastliest chapters in the annals of history. Senseless persecutions, outbursts of hate and brutality are only a few of the manifestations of a civilization that is beset with dread and terror. When reason is weakened by the forces of panic and dismay, events of tragic and uncontrollable dimensions become more probable. Dead yesterdays and unborn tomorrows mark the trail of frenzied emotions and human fright. Present dilemmas are stirred up not only by the malice of the few but by an all-encompassing climate of fear. Like pestilences of old, terrors unchecked destroy our creative responses of life.

Although many of our fears are justified, some of them lack solid foundation. Phobias, irrational aversions, upset our inner balance without outer justifications. Close places, high places, open places, obsessive fears of animals, pain or death are but a few of the indications that an individual has lost emotional control. Illogical feelings of dread affect not only the freedom of choice but also the liberty of action. An otherwise normal person filled with exaggerated inhibitions can respond almost automatically with strange patterns of behavior. Even when phobia-prone individuals understand that the panic is caused by reasons of the imagination, they still are not able to cope with the situation. In addition to a calm and thoughtful attitude, a serious attempt to follow professional guidance and a gentle manner induced by self-discipline can be the most essential steps to healing.

Present world conditions, characterized by persistent upheavals and turmoil, contribute to the widespread dangers of fear. Human nature is made insecure with chaos. Most of us function reasonably well when we know what to expect and what is expected of us. Our times of transition remove a long-accustomed security and force us to face situations for which we are insufficiently prepared. An unknown tomorrow throws suspicions on the potential of today. A civilization based on law and order fosters a sense of trust, whereas culture arising from disorder disrupts the security needed to envision a better tomorrow.

Amidst individual worries and perplexities, we are never more disturbed than when our pride is hurt by a critical judgment, review or observation. The inner sanctum of our character, the self, does not welcome an exposure of its weaknesses and inhibitions. Vanities and conceit, so strong a part of the human condition, thrive in a world that flatters our hidden and open desires. What a delight for us when our achievements are applauded! Isn't praise manna for the soul? Even mediocre talent will rise to a greater height when encouraged by word or deed. A just and fair criticism offered for the sake of improvement surely plays a positive role in the development of human achievement. On the other hand, criticism unduly harsh or unwarranted can destroy future efforts to excel.

Self-honesty does not come painlessly. Few of us have the capacity to judge ourselves with exactness. To accept reality, even in its extremes, without sensing the need to falsify it in accordance with our desires is the best testament to our maturity. Anyone who allows illusion to shape the mental picture of thoughts and ideas prepares for a world that does not exist. Only those of us able to gauge our competence and deficiencies without continuous, anxious concern will gain a balanced view of society. Humility becomes a virtue when it can dispense with self-exultation and debasement.

"It is appointed unto man to die." Rarely have so few words stirred up so many fears. Although few people are foolish enough to argue about the inescapability of death, some of the aspects of our final demise cause great worry. In the face of death we are confronted with physical changes that are inevitable yet repulsive. Deterioration in any form is not a pleasant thought. The prospect of disappearing as a "person" does not make the idea of death more engaging. Since we are so deeply attached to material enjoyments, we find it difficult to persuade our mind to look forward to a time of spiritual pleasures alone.

Even while dying, we cling to life. Although divine revelation assures us of many heavenly treasures, we question whether we will be among those received by God. In addition, the alternative to heaven can become such a heavy burden on our souls that the thought of death distorts the legitimate joys on earth, undermines our confidence and adds terror to the torment. To be lost without ever being found again is for many of us the greatest fear of all.

People hesitate to speak to the living about the fear of dying and certainly that is excusable, but not to mention death to a suffering friend who seeks enlightenment can be an act lacking in courage. Unquestionably, the possibility of dying makes discussion difficult; it is a great disservice, however, to withhold the truth from someone struggling to prepare for the end of life. Regardless of good intentions, when we assure a friend or relative on the threshold of death that everything is fine, our efforts to camouflage reality is still the thoughtless lie. More often than not, a terminal patient is ready and even anxious to accept the unavoidable news, especially when the words are spoken with comforting and loving concern. Shared prayer and a demonstration of deep faith can generate such power and confidence that the patient is able to lay aside many timid emotions.

Worries over the subject of death fall and rise with the importance we invest in our own existence here on earth. When we realize, intellectually and emotionally, that life in its very essence is finite, we are in a position to accept the idea of death. Anyone who considers this present state on earth as the ultimate, however, can be so overly attached to comfortable living habits that the very notion of surrendering these comforts grows unbearable. Although Holy Scripture warns us that earth is not a lasting city, most of us give little attention to such teachings.

Since there is much in us that is afraid of truth, there remains much in us that is afraid of God. The real and the unchangeable with their uncompromising consequences unsettle our customary life-styles. Inherent weaknesses in the structure of our personality induce us to favor the pleasing over the disagreeable. When attitudes regarding positions and privileges are not in full accord with the pure and simple message preached by our Redeemer, selfish ambitions take over. For fear of the human, people support causes that oppose divine commands. Many of the poor, disabled and ignorant are shunned or mistreated in spite of all the examples given to us by Christ and His Apostles. This is not to imply that everything we do is wrong; it is just a strong reminder that we don't always do everything right. Too many people are willing to go quickly along their way without taking an exact account of their conscience. Some prefer to delay confrontations with truth until they grow older and more sensitive to the final reflections on life, but others induced by fear often work toward salvation by asking Christ to forgive the presence of weakness.

The calm needed to lift our spirits can be drawn only from sources found within the self. Faith, hope, and our fear of offending God will provide the strength to deny some of our more impetuous emotions and control the rush of our sensuous appetite. By accepting and acknowledging our divine heritage, we grow receptive to the need of linking external activities with inner inspirations. Since the love of God is unconditional, our sins and miseries do not erect a barrier between us and our Redeemer. A *God loved* can also be a *God feared.* Aren't we all afraid of offending a person close to our heart?

Fear, a problem that leaves hardly a life untouched, offers everyone the same lesson: *reach out for help.* Not many people are in a position to face the vicissitudes of life completely on their own strength. Fueled by a disturbed imagination, anxieties will disrupt the balance of a person who is alone. When surrounded by friends, he has access to a mysterious reservoir of courage and daring that is not reachable by the person who is alone. It is possible for one friend to persuade another that apprehensions need not threaten to the point of surrender. By appealing to inner fortitude, even the timid personality is able to perform wonders. When we are reminded of others who have conquered adversity, the convic-

tion "If they did it, so can I" becomes a determined motivation. In the end, the knowledge that we are supported by
compassion and love eases the burden of all possible hardships. "For where two or three meet in my name, I shall be
there with them" (Matt. 18:20).

Too many people are slow to ask for help. Some are afraid
that they will impose, and others are too proud to admit
their needs. Love, by its very nature, yearns to show itself
in action, and yet friends cannot affirm their sympathy and
affection if they are never given the chance. Is there any act
more revealing and rewarding than the desire to assist a
friend? All of us have close acquaintances who would welcome the opportunity to prove their true nature; "love asked
for" more often than not allows love to happen. How can
we discover the value of our friends unless our needs test
their integrity and honor? To presume that people are unwilling to offer their support shows a pessimistic view of
amity.

Situations that engender fear carry within themselves latent seeds of a possible solution. When a personal upset leaves
us with sadness and painful suspicions, a deep longing arises
within our hearts to revive the sense of trust once again.
Those of us who are conscious of the fact that fears unchecked produce even greater consternation have the responsibility to neutralize the cause of the initial predicament. Our divine Creator gave us, along with His cross, the
corresponding grace to bear it. We have been told that no
one will ever be tested beyond personal strength, but there
remains the question of whether anyone links this divine
assurance with daily experiences. Through love and inspiration, God's chosen beings are empowered to employ the
skills and labor that will transform the barren land of fear
into a harvest of trust. Constancy of faith and never-ending
hope help to quiet our agitations and misgivings. When difficult hours of life are translated into the fruitful challenge,
fears can be conquered with moral courage. The human
triumph which then emerges affects not only our individual
well-being but also the quality of our relationships with friends
and neighbors.

Jesus, foretelling His agony and death, prayed to His heavenly Father: "Now my soul is troubled. What shall I say: Father, save me from this hour? But it was for this very reason that I have come to this hour. Father, glorify your name" (John 12:27–28). Our Savior, human in everything except sin, set His face toward the passion as the ultimate price of redemption. His will followed the will of His heavenly Father. The agony of fear and the emptying of self were in great measure responsible for the opening of the gate to life everlasting. By responding to fear with dependence and love, Christ turned aside pain and submitted to the plan of salvation. "Unto thy hands I commit my spirit."

Christ experienced Good Friday and the splendor of Easter in order to give us an example to follow. The Head of the mystical body has prepared the way we are destined to take. Dismay and consternation may continue to invade our lives, but when kept in perspective with His plan, they shall never become masters of human destiny. Fears, as overwhelming as they may be, have the mysterious capacity to direct all men, women and children toward the maturity and greatness yet to be accomplished. That which starts in fear can be made to end in triumph!

Chapter 10

LISTENING

It takes a bit of listening
To hear the spoken word,
Sometimes the very things I've said
Are not what you have heard.

To empty the self and leave the mind free for the sake of another one's fulfillment, that is listening. A desire to parade our insights and wisdom are silenced so that the ideas and wishes of another move toward the center of our attention. An exchange takes place between a conquered self and the needy one. For a period of time our own urgencies are postponed to allow the overflow of apprehensions and joys of the "other" find a secure haven in our heart. When we are totally present to the word of another, when our heart and mind participate in what is being said and what is not mentioned, we assure our friend that someone is close by, someone who is willing to listen. The weary pilgrim finds a well-earned rest in the shadow of our soul.

Undoubtedly, physical presence is an essential ingredient in the art of listening, but it alone cannot guarantee success. We can be present in a room with our heart far away. People living together can be worlds apart. In order to listen well, we have to add our spiritual riches and mental assets to the process of understanding so that listening becomes an inner experience and not only an outer performance. With our ears we hear; with our hearts we listen. When our sensitivities and emotions are mobilized and fully alerted to the needs of others, we are best prepared to perceive the message they are so eager to convey. The "I listen" becomes identical with "I am with you; I understand what you are telling me and together we will face the problem."

In spite of its frequency and universal appeal, the art of listening is not decorated with all the graces it deserves. More than half of our communications, whether of an economic, political or diplomatic nature, are easily ignored, misunderstood or quickly forgotten. Individual experiences confirm the fact that the capacity to listen is on the decline. How eager we are to capitalize on every opportunity to speak and how rarely do we look for opportunities to let other people add their thoughts! Our preference to pay attention to ourselves preoccupies us so much that the weaknesses endured by others are forgotten. The greater the "ego," the tinier the "you."

Listening is not yet on the way to its grave. As a national pastime, "concern for others" receives such a poor rating that we may soon reach the point of crisis. As a personal need, however, it is still the most potent force in the intricate network of human understanding. Along with the psychiatrist, there are concerned parents, religious leaders and counselors who silence their own questions in order to grasp better the adversities and afflictions borne by others. Listening is severely tested by men and women who pay little attention to the needs of others, but to predict the demise of listening is a premature gesture not substantiated by reality. Those of us who are interested in the moral perceptions of our neighbors have a duty to convince others that listeners and speakers alike are responsible for the truth. Only then will we accord to both individuals the respect they deserve.

The mind was not born to sit still. The words "here, there and everywhere" describe accurately the various excursions that our mental capacities and emotional longings undertake. An inquisitive and restless curiosity aiming to stir the unknown finds it laborious to focus on one subject alone. A multitude of happenings knock at our door looking for attention, asking to be heard and answered. It takes a serious effort and thoughtful patience to be totally present and absorbed in the tales of woe other people need to unburden. If we possess the enviable capacity for listening, we are destined to be friends and helpers; if we cannot discipline our inner impetuosities and favor the speaker, we are not yet able to heal through listening.

An "in-built" obstacle to letting another person speak is the fact that the mind is quicker than the tongue. Between the word spoken and the word understood, a remarkable time difference exerts noteworthy influence on our desire to listen. When one person's speech is slow and meaningless, the other person's intelligence can be forced into a painful vacuum in which the mind becomes anxious and restless. Thoughts can wander far when magnets of attraction are not in sight! To become fidgety with an annoying orator is not a sign of impatience but a vigorous testimony to the liveliness of the listener's spirit. When delivery lacks fire and excitement, the speaker runs the risk that some people will choose sleep as one way out of the embarrassing dilemma.

To assume that listening is effortless contradicts prevailing opinions of people who make a profession of counseling with "ear and heart." Hard work, draining and exhausting, is an accurate description of the professional listener's day in the heavily frequented office. Medical reports claim that paying attention to others increases the beat of the heart, raises the temperature and uses up more energy than manual labor. I am "tired of listening" refers not only to psychological reactions but also to the physical condition of the one who has spent many hours in human dialogue. Is it any wonder that we single out friends, *not* acquaintances, when we look for someone to hearken to our complaints and revelations? In the heart of a friend we expect to find the emotional and intellectual identity needed to unburden our soul. Strangers who hear only our words deepen our loneliness, whereas people who understand our thoughts lighten our hearts. How gladly we listen to those we love even when they have little to say. Affection is more eloquent than reason.

Selective listening is ill-conceived if it is based on the other's personal charm or an emotional attraction. Preferences are understandable, of course, but likes and dislikes should never be so strong that our loyalty to truth is influenced. To allow the outer appearance of a speaker to sway our judgment removes our critical reliability and inner trust. The thought may be difficult to accept, but it is true that people we shower with affection do not always present a subject any better than someone we find unlikeable. Issues, not the images reflected in our hearts, must remain at the core of our discussions. How can we grow in knowledge if we block out the stimulation of new ideas? Our frantic search for solutions in our world-wide predicaments need leaders especially chosen for their redeeming insights, not their high media ratings. "Do not praise a man for his good looks, nor dislike anybody for his appearance" (Eccles.11:2).

Not all of our feelings can be translated into speech; the unspoken message also wants to be heard. Our emotions dig in so deeply and carve out such a maze of secret passageways and labyrinths of escape that words cannot reveal the full intensity of human conquest. Facial expressions, lively gestures, studied hesitations and elegant pauses can appeal to our listening capacities in far more compelling ways than any eloquence of speech. Perhaps just as many lives are saved or improved by spontaneous looks of sympathy and friendship as are saved through surgical procedures. Next to the doctor who heals with medical attention, a place must be left for the priest who seeks to heal through listening.

Silence does not always express an unwillingness to speak. People who have much to say, yet lack the art of saying it, may strike us as being incommunicative, but this may not always be the case. It could be inhibitions and hidden guilt that lame the tongue. The wearing of a mask is not necessarily reprehensible; the make-believe can be the last means of self-protection and survival. Can we blame people who hide things with which they have not yet learned to live? How true the popular saying, "Don't be fooled by the face I show for I wear a thousand masks and none show who I am!"

Everyday our ears are deluged with a continuous flood of

sounds, and it is up to us to select what is important enough to retain and remember. By choosing "quality" we are not overpowered by "quantity." If we do not acquire a taste of our own, the taste of others will regulate our priorities. Naturally, the stressful situations of our loved ones take precedence, because husbands and wives, parents and children develop an interdependence of feelings and emotions that need to be sustained by the frequent exchange of tenderness. Listening to one another's imagination, hopes and sufferings is the best way of confirming unity. Whenever we sever our willingness to be mentally present to those in need, we deny the sacred duty of imitating the Good Samaritan. In the final analysis, the greatest crisis experienced by our families today is the failure to listen to one another with real attention. To force a person into silence can destroy the spirit.

Speakers in our modern civilization will be more successful if they consider the fact that audiences usually are surprisingly strong in knowledge. Even specialists who discuss their findings on certain research projects are amazed at how much their listeners know about that particular subject. The time when ignorance of the masses was presumed has long vanished, due perhaps to the interest and appeal of modern education. When a speaker takes this into account and treats the audience respectfully on equal terms, those who came to listen become ardent followers. Undoubtedly, groups of people can be impolite, even offensive, but in their hearts even they know the difference between a message of conceit and a delivery of humility and truth.

Too many details can lessen the effectiveness of a speech. A fragmented delivery of a theory that is interrupted time and again with a number of proofs and counterproofs leaves the listener in a state of bewilderment. The person confused with details quickly withdraws concentration from the main topic of discussion. Obviously, to stress a point makes it clear; to repeat it too often defeats its purpose. The attention span of an uncommitted assembly of people who came to learn reaches its limits when explanations become repetitious. The witty speaker who generates interest is seldom greeted with a yawn. Anyone able to compress the greatest presentation of thoughts into the smallest presentation of words will be rewarded with the honor of receiving "capacity attention."

Technical progress with its triumphant sweep over the old-fashioned way of communicating has damaged our desire and need to dialogue and listen. A people sated with headphones, computers and television sets frown on any effort to reach out to each other and establish the "personal touch." The entertainment media are so pervasive that our attempts to share "sounds and self" have little chance of prevailing against the magic of the tube. Our exciting home video systems have started a gigantic upheaval that alters all previously established patterns of general interest and family behavior. The human being usually at the center of attention is easily replaced by channels turned off and on by the volatile touch of a finger. Sharing memories, exchanging experiences and enjoying personal humor are now replaced with impersonal programs that enter the home over invisible waves. The "other," in need or not, is reduced to a marginal character, near enough not to be forgotten yet too remote to receive our attention. The antenna, so proudly dominating the various shapes of the rooftops, has dealt a serious blow to our attitudes toward one another. "Prime time" is the new direction!

Progress should not be indicted as the main culprit in our difficulties of relating and listening to one another. Inventions as startling as televisions and computers are not connected with any set of moral values. It is our attitude, our response that allows the good or evil into the sanctuary of our homes. We are the ones who freely decide which programs will invade the privacy of our families and friends. Public laws can only restrict or prevent temptations and vulgarity. Our moral convictions are the ultimate guardians that protect our own conscience and the well-being of our youth. It is our own fault if we permit entertainment media to become the undisputed masters in our homes. When trivial shows make us forget our duties toward others, and friends are disavowed for interrupting a miniseries, then moral precepts have already yielded to the fancy of the screen. When entertainment is restricted to the inevitable moments of physical or mental fatigue, however, the distraction can give welcome relief and lighten the burdens of an exacting day.

As seeds petition fertile soil to root and blossom, so do our ears and hearts request a land of stillness and peace in order to perceive the messages of our friends and acquaintances. Pandemonium can drain our reservoirs of energy to such a degree that we become listless and weary when others expect us to be concerned and sympathetic. In a state of war with ourselves, we communicate more unrest and strife. God, who dwells in the depths of our being, waits patiently for the arrival of serenity and calm. "Be still," He commands, "and know that I am your God." Unless the waves of the stormy sea settle down and rest, it is difficult for us to hear God or feel His presence. The quiet hours, the secret places where strains and tensions find release, are destined to become times of waiting upon the Lord. When the hush of silence and tranquillity restores our strength and replenishes our resilience, we are empowered to listen without being weary. Obviously, stillness is not able to lift all the curtains of distress or solve all the riddles of mankind; it does, however, advance the promise of renewed courage and hope so that we are able to rise above the dangerous clouds of panic and fear. The moment we sense and experience the healing effects of stillness, our capacity to listen increases and deepens.

Occasionally, a kind of pouting between friends take place when God berates us for not listening to Him and we complain that He doesn't hear us either. We cannot understand why God is so distant, and God is bemused by our futile efforts to program Him. We find the heavenly treatment of silence almost unacceptable, and God considers petitions uttered with domineering presumption to be out of character for people who depend entirely on His divine provisions. And so it goes, each department issuing complaints and warnings to which neither pays much attention.

GOD:

"And I did tell you, but you would not listen, and you rebelled against the voice of Yahweh" (Deut. 1:43).

"They have reverted to the crimes of their ancestors who refused to listen to my words" (Jer. 11:10).

"I will not listen when they call to me in the time of their distress" (Jer. 11:14).

"If they fast, I will not listen to their plea" (Jer. 14:12).

WE:

"I cry to you, and you give me no answer; I stand before you, but you take no notice" (Job 30:20).

"Listen, only listen to my words; this is the consolation you can offer me" (Job 21:1–2).

"God, hear my cry for help, listen to my prayer!" (Ps. 61:1–2).

"How long, Yahweh, am I to cry for help while you will not listen; to cry 'Oppression' in your ear and you will not save?" (Hab. 1–2).

Among people who need each other, a difference of opinion can serve to animate the bonds of trust and affection; real love does not diminish at the presence of an occasional rift. Feelings usually intensify after a storm has calmed. Moments of disappointment between friends do not advocate separation; they clarify the conditions on which the friendship rests. After our Lord has stated His case and we have shown Him ours, the air is cleared and our hearts are emptied of antagonism, leaving us really free to listen to each other again. "Where can we go, Master, when you alone bring to our ears words of everlasting life?"

Chapter 11

PREJUDICE

Hate scars the mind with prejudice,
A mask of heartless vision,
It speaks in tongues of thoughtlessness
Pretending sound decision.

Prejudice is one of our most perturbing phenomena. The persistent styles of prejudgment of people because they are different have an adverse effect on the quality and sincerity of human relationships. Religious convictions not in tune with our own, unpleasant social conditions, and human characteristics we dislike are things that put caution and distance on immediate alert. Without making an attempt to get to know the individual involved, we set up invisible barriers that cause resentment. People are blamed for their heritage and for circumstances over which they have never had control.

In our early years, most of us were taught to respect the integrity and dignity of the human being and to relate to everyone with equal innocence and joy. As the child approaches adulthood, however, animosities can develop toward people who do not fit into the narrow definition of acceptability. Very often those who match natural expectations are favored, whereas others who lack approval are neglected. Studied courtesies and cool reserve edge out the warmth of trust. The "love one another" gradually changes into "beware."

The mind made up is impervious to truth just as curtains drawn shut out the light. Closed mentalities, convinced of their righteousness, are rarely in a mood to listen to arguments that originate on the opposite side; knowing all the answers, they find different opinions irrelevant. When they are pressured by decisions contrary to their own, their arguments detail particular personal experiences and that ends the discussion! Usually such discriminatory behavior thrives on ignorance, and the unwillingness to change or even to listen demonstrates that the conditions will never improve. Life in its spontaneous newness is forced to submit to a mind without hope.

In contrast to the self-induced ignorant, there are many serious-minded intellectuals totally receptive to ever-changing experiences and insights. Knowledge open to growth remains aware of the fact that absolute certainty in any real life situation is beyond reach. Doubt is not only an integral part of living, it is also an ever-present force in progress. Scientists and theologians as well have an obligation to check their discoveries well before their conclusions are made public. Not many in our midst can afford to say that their opinions are final. Have we forgotten how much we learn from our mistakes? Even the most stunning achievement had to walk the way of error.

The tendency to discriminate cannot be viewed as an isolated factor. Private enterprises, public institutions and associations of every kind condone attitudes that offend great numbers of people. Far too often the disadvantaged, weak and abandoned are given less consideration than human dignity deserves. The person with an average income is apt to be considered less important than the one with material wealth. Whenever status symbols are used as the ultimate mark of respectability, some very special people are overlooked. Classifications are able to describe only the outer wrappings of a character; it takes sympathy and love to discover the inner world of the individual. Today, men and women in ever-growing numbers are defying the unethical norms of prejudice and are building relationships based on their own judgments of goodness. In choosing this less-traveled road as their path through life, they are rewarded with sincere and honorable companions.

Discrimination is not of heavenly origin. Forming a strong opinion without good reason against someone or something is a flaw in the development of our characters. Such leanings of the mind are not inborn; they are acquired by milieu, education and individual experiences. Children, by their very nature carefree and tolerant, associate with one another in a spontaneous and graceful manner. Unaware of barriers erected by the sophisticated adult, they make no attempt to distinguish among faces and colors. Joy and sorrow are the factors that matter. It is later on, as the growing years teach an overpowering self-importance and the ability to pretend, that traits of jealousy and hate are added to the personality. When one's feelings are hurt by an individual of a particular nationality or race, a wall of distrust is built up against other people of that same group. Suspicions pester the thoughts as love grows cold. Humans, instead of God, become the arbiters of who is going to be loved and who is going to be hated. Personal earthly censorship lays a heavy curtain of mistrust over a world struggling with dissent. Is it any wonder that when asked to define the essence of humanity, our Lord simply requested "Be like this child"?

Many prejudices arise when knowledge is faulty and thoughts are incomplete. The less we know about another person's motives, hopes and dreams, the greater the margin of error in our thinking. When we are familiar with the thoughts and ideas of people around us, we gladly seek their company in order to share the common treasure. It is the unknown that perplexes us; it is the stranger who is shunned. The frightening ghettos not only restrict our physical movements, they also constrain the flow of affection from our heart. Fences, invisible or not, foster suspicions and antipathy.

Regardless of how simply the disparities begin, the longer the separation is allowed to exist, the deeper the abyss engulfs itself in ignorance. Our military conflicts are fought by people who never get to know one another, and so it is with our personal conflicts. Wouldn't all of our confrontations have a better chance at early settlement if the individuals involved would make a serious effort to learn how the other person feels? The handshake of cordiality, "I'd like to know you better," makes a friend of the stranger. The more a nation strengthens its education in respectability, the less the chance that discrimination will grow. Not that perceptions of honor alone will solve all disputes, but the presence of truth is an encouraging sign of good will.

Bias is an inhibiting factor in personal relationships and equally so in our alliances with other nations. Judging the value of different countries based on our slanted views and personal thoughts forces an uncertain and perhaps false impression. Preconceived suspicions have little difficulty in justifying their validity. On the other hand, however, an open, unbiased mind discovers testimonies of love and understanding and allows the erroneous assumptions to be qualified.

The objective mind, unattached to folklore and long-established opinions, is the safest guarantee of truth. When the thoughts and theories preferred by other nations are made clear, they have a right to be pondered on merit rather than on presumed opinions. The implied supposition that all people should behave in a fashion pleasing to our ideals fails to take into account the inalienable right of each country to determine its own destiny. Diversity in the manner of action and reaction is a credit to the element of variety in God's masterful creation. How unbearable is the specter of a universe wherein everyone recites from the same script!

People unable to face reality are easily tempted to falsify conditions in order to be able to cope with certain situations. Their views are narrowed and minds imprisoned due to flaws in mental comprehension or because of the disapproval of actions that do not match their own. To see only what they want to see blinds them to the fascinating marvels of the world. Although an individual is not expected to know everything, there should always be the desire to seek available opportunities to learn. Talents given by God were meant to be multiplied. Usually, the person who claims to "know it already" is less informed than the person who begs for knowledge. How great is the joy "to discover and learn"!

Our needs of today are served with respectful listening, not prejudicial discussions. By allowing a friend or neighbor the chance to speak, we assume an obligation to listen with patience. Dictatorial political systems that enforce blind submission inflict upon themselves a mediocrity of thought and action. Whenever people pretend that they cannot gain in knowledge from another culture or civilization, they add shame to ignorance. Respect for the spiritual and mental riches that prevail in other lands is more than a diplomatic courtesy, it is also an acknowledgement that out of diversity emerges real unity.

The right to personal opinions, so loudly proclaimed today, includes the unheralded duty to educate ourselves to the best of our means. Information classified as traditional may be correct and yet only partially true. If public theories and judgments offered by word or example do not agree with personal ideas of justice and love, we have a responsibility to search for more satisfactory solutions. Although it may be painful to disengage ourselves from a long-honored heritage, such action often initiates remarkable progress and success. To question past teachings with wisdom and caution speaks with more honesty than the response of *yes* given in fear. A process of unlearning may be necessary before we are able to learn again.

Communication is a most effective way to prevent prejudice and discrimination; good dialogue helps to remove a variety of suspicions. Isn't it in speaking together that people come together? When interests are shared in conversation, class distinctions are loosened and affections are strengthened; the rightly spoken word serves as a healing bridge.

To converse is to disclose. Insights as well as intuitions rarely gleaned from other sources reveal themselves in the course of a communion of thought and inspiration. Without the beneficial effects of a sincere and open discussion, the hopes and desires of another individual cannot be correctly analyzed. What appeared first as an irritation moves into an entirely different light when it is fully understood. More than once has conversation offered a shelter against diffidence and despair.

The state of soundlessness parades in many disguises. The unpleasant silence held too long because of misunderstandings or ill treatment can cause prejudices to form and grow well beyond reparation. Strong-willed people choose to be taciturn because they cannot withdraw their feelings of revenge. Others are not given to conversation since they consider most listeners are below par. The umbrella of silence, covering a multitude of sins, shields ignorance and small festering hurts. Some people have to diminish others in order to exalt themselves. When preoccupation with personal concerns takes precedence over the anxieties of others, the accompanying self-importance takes over and the needs of companions appear minor and unworthy. Biased opinions are not created by actions but by the mind and attitudes that allow prejudices to branch out and deepen. Even when the deportment of acquaintances arouses anger, it is really our own thoughts that summon suspicion and hate. Habitual patterns and emotional reactions are the fertile breeding grounds for the growth of twisted partiality. Our fate is written not in the stars but in the mysterious corners of our character where ultimate decisions are forged and sanctioned. What becomes a serious part of thinking gradually makes up the serious part of self.

Between the wastelands of arrogance and conceit lies the virtue of humility. The truly humble man or woman is not able to act with biased intentions. Exaltation of self at the expense of others is alien to a mind that is fully conscious of limitations and liabilities. Attempts to raise ourselves above others are denials of the circumstances into which we were born and in which we must die. With our less than perfect origin in mind, how can we confront another human being with insolence and pride? "If our life in Christ means anything to you, if love can persuade at all, or the Spirit we have in common, or any tenderness and sympathy, then beunited in your convictions and united in your love, with a common purpose and a common mind" (Phil. 2:1–2).

Because humility, the most potent force against prejudice, is discussed more than practiced, it receives only a cautious nod of approval. Such a quality must endure the test of life in order to prove that it is more fact than fiction. Actions and words assume so many masks that the "real" grows beyond recognition. Weaknesses paraded as virtue make the casual observer suspicious. Since modesty and submissive gestures are not always followed by convincing deeds, a world grown skeptical prefers to wait for social interactions of quality before it renders judgment. Unfortunately, pure humility that mirrors the total surrender of self is rare; such people are exceptional. For almost all of us, the ideal remains distant, a continuing battle against many odds.

Perfection in any field is not easy to achieve, and it may be too idealistic to expect the total elimination of prejudice from our present civilization. But *not yet* should never be extended into the categorical *never*. Justice, the eternal law that keeps humanity civilized, must never be sacrificed simply to perpetuate inequality. Citizens who still treasure responsibility will never rest until conditions are established for every human being to be treated in like manner. This is a sacred task that has yet to be accomplished. Until these prerequisites of fairness and equity are secured by laws and better living patterns, no one should become complacent or neutral. The person who claims ignorance or noninvolvement is really registering a silent plea of guilt.

Fortunately, not every step in life directs us to fall. What has been done can be undone. An arrogant pattern of prejudice, even the most repulsive act of bigotry, need not be the final testimony of men or women anxious for successful human encounters. A chance for improvement is always present. Certainly our world is not perfect, but to make it as perfect as humanly possible is the most sacred mission on earth. God created each one of us to succeed, not to fail.

When God looked at the being He so carefully created, He

found the human to be "good"; and good, very good indeed we are. The capacity to reason, the willingness to strive, the ability to love, the readiness to forgive and express compassion make us the undisputed rulers of God's majestic universe. But how many of us recognize the equality of our neighbors and truly enjoy the amenities in our relationships with one another? Only when there is growth in this oneness of spirit will the seeds of splendor implanted by the divine Gardener have a chance to break through the hardened crust of social barriers. Instead of weeping over the results of prejudice, shouldn't we be rejoicing that with our help it can be conquered?

Chapter 12

LET BE

*I love you friend just as you are
Enough to let you be,
And when my several faults appear
Please do the same for me.*

Fascinating is the majesty of our mighty mountains as they reach with colossal might into the white billows of clouds. Exhilarating is the roaring sea, surging and recoiling with boundless fury only to calm down again with gentleness and peace. Enchanting is the delight of colorful flowers as they sprinkle their innocence and perfume over the face of the lovely meadows. Brilliant is the glitter of stars that embellish the lines of our endless skies. Can anything compare with this splendid array of nature's grandeur and beauty? Is there anything more impressive and more moving than the reflections of God's magnificent creation? Yes, there is; of course there is. The one thing more captivating, more enchanting than any of the priceless excitements of nature is the created being, the person called *you*, the person called *me*.

For us, God has more love in His heart than for all the mountains, waters and flowers. God has more affection and feeling for each one of us than for all the changing shades of the seasons. Why did God put His very best into the creation of the human being? Was it necessary for the human species to be of such incredible variety when far less would have been equally satisfactory to us? Obviously, in God's mind it *was* necessary because God loves us and divine love cannot be limited. When God fashioned the image of the human being, His only thought was one of "greatness." "Slightly less than God" was the position He reserved for the human family. Everyone had to be different, unique, not two the same, a reflection of divine riches and divine imagination. In every sense of the word, His love toward us was unconditional. It was His intention to give us the freedom "to be."

"As I have loved you, so you have to love each other." God asks us to imitate His generosity in our exchanges of affection. Our love for Him and for one another is expected to reflect His care, solicitude and greatness. We too are invited to give abundantly in unsurpassed measure, with little thought of self, even to the point of giving up our life so that another one can survive.

How are we doing in this regard? Is our love genuine and inspired by sincere motivations? Can we see the image of the Divine in our friends, or are they enjoyed simply because they add to our satisfaction? Do the demands we make on them curtail their freedom or is their individuality open to development? Questions like these encourage us to reflect on the quality of our affections and the integrity of our minds. Accepting our friends and neighbors as they are, which often means different, suggests that we are free from coercion and conceit. If self-scrutiny reveals that we allow people to be themselves only so long as they please us, our "love" is really a camouflaged interest in the self. The concerns of others mean very little when we are steeped in the needs of our egos. Love that is worthy of trust gauges the interest of the loved one with the same sincerity that it weighs its own.

Yielding to others the liberty to "be" presupposes our readiness to bear patiently with their less-attractive qualities. The disappointing sides of friends have also to be taken into account. If we love only what we like in their personalities, we succumb to an image and fail to discover reality. By letting them "be," we find splendor and shadow mingled together into one. The challenge rests in our understanding of the pleasant or unpleasant and still being able to go on loving. With our own frustrations about imperfections, of not being what we want to be, how can we demand others to give a more agreeable performance? Only when we can accept and live with both imperfection and perfection are we mature enough for the long-lasting friendship of love.

Our ability to let other people be offers them the privilege and freedom to venture out and live fully their individual characters and styles. Regardless of whether particular features are considered noble or weak, our willingness to accept those around us as they are grants them the right to act naturally in every situation. Far from stifling our self-expression, this act of sympathy and understanding provides an atmosphere of openness and harmony. The diversities of opinion and the possibilities of contradiction are not only endured but also recognized as valid and necessary in every human interaction. Tolerance removes the sting attached to the reactions of the obstinate.

Letting ourselves be, the acceptance of ourselves as we are, is an equally important factor of life. We play the fool when we expect life to serve a constant accolade of praise and honor. Although the ceremonial embrace marking the recognition of an outstanding achievement can be the unforgettable "once-in-a-lifetime" experience, it is self-defeating to expect the limelight to be our constant companion. Daily routine does not lend itself to the glamour of the extraordinary performance. We are born to strive and to excel, but it is obvious that the reality of our actions rarely matches the quality of our dreams. Whether we like it or not, weaknesses inherent in our nature force most of our activities to remain ordinary.

Growth is seldom painless. To let ourselves be, without labels or categories, means to say *yes* to that part of our inner development that is filled with pain and disappointment. The winding road to genuine self-acceptance and real self-esteem is not only long and tiring, but risky and dangerous as well. When vanity and selfishness confuse our intentions, it may be difficult to be satisfied with the "self" that God created for us.

Obviously, since human nature is not flawless, mistakes and disappointments will inevitably follow the human trail. Errors made are not so much a regrettable oversight as they are an integral part of nature. Shuttling back and forth over the troubled waters of life makes us prone to faulty connections and wrong numbers. Our complex universe questions us far beyond our ability to answer. Since so much of our knowledge is tentative, open to correction and amendment, truth is probably considered more common in heaven than on earth.

In addition to the occasional mental lapses we all experience, physical conditions such as exhaustion and fatigue inhibit the accuracy of our thoughts. When the flesh is lacking in vitality, the mind is lacking in precision and exactness. Fortunately, few of our mistakes are made on purpose. Some of them are signs of our feebleness, weakness and poor concentration. Although they are negative forces in the summary of human expression, they serve a very positive mission by pointing out the many areas in which we still have a lot to learn. The presumption that we know it all is quickly shattered when we are confronted with our wrong judgments and inaccurate conclusions. Hardly anything serves humility better than our blunders. Poor decisions that show us the need for study and counsel can easily become the proverbial blessings in disguise. A momentary embarrassment can be painful indeed, but this very embarrassment can be the catalyst to our next success. Only the stubborn and incorrigible are willing to repeat their misdeeds without drawing any profit from them.

Professional critics in the fields of art and entertainment are paid to decry a poor performance. They offer a necessary service. There are other people, however, who act as "self-appointed" judges, intent on indicting others from a personal standpoint without reflecting on their own idiosyncrasies. Their comments cause more harm with one sentence than others do in a book! Why are they so eager to unmask mistakes? Is it a passion for truth or can it be a concealed way of lifting personal inner frustrations and disappointments? By seeing in their friends and neighbors the things they hate in themselves, they become critics of their own jealousy rather than critics of truth.

Mistakes are not always disastrous. The ones we allow "to be" harm us less than the mistakes we try to conceal. Whatever we hide is apt to fester. By acting innocently when we know we are guilty, we damage our personal reputation as much as our inner integrity. To profess in gesture and speech that we are *not guilty*, even when faced with condemning evidence, projects an appearance of outer calm and hides the inner storm and chaos. An alliance between the outer front and the inner spirit has to be forged before maturity and character have a chance to grow.

Some people work against the "self" by magnifying personal faults and by refusing to forgive their own carelessness. Others, more resourceful, minimize their poor performances to such a degree that they appear almost virtuous. The nightmare of one is a mere miscalculation for the other. Temperaments react in different ways: what the pessimist never forgets, the optimist hardly remembers. The calamity howler begins to worry before the problem comes into existence, and the person of hope refuses to recognize a problem even when it may exist! Overreaction is natural for adults whose false steps of early childhood were harshly treated; for the child who was shielded from blame, however, overconfidence may become a domineering aspect of the personality.

Since time heals wounds as well as disappointments, all is not lost when a mistake is made. With ingenuity and determination, we can make sure that our daily appraisals come closer to the truth and that decisions are made in honesty. By familiarizing ourselves with the benefits of calm and patience, we can avoid actions of haste, one of the eminent causes of our foolish blunders. If hurried speech causes most of our troubles, second thoughts can be considered before we offer our opinions. Should forgetfulness be our downfall, our minds can be trained to become more reliable and disciplined. This is not to suggest that efforts of this kind will eliminate all future mistakes; it simply offers the hope that by letting ourselves be, we will learn to recognize our faults and strive to correct them.

Many of us are able to go along in life more or less placidly and let our mistakes "be" until suddenly we are upset by an unexpected collapse of our dreams. Certainly the thought of being wiped out financially or of losing our reputation is not a pleasant one. Yet even when a serious failure drives us to the edge of hopelessness, we have to learn to adjust in order to prevent a greater affliction. No one succeeds in everything; some of the things we do will come to triumph and others will be destined to fail. It is a sign of real greatness to be able to interact with both success and failure without being subdued by either. The one whose life is totally dependent upon success will lose confidence at the first sign of disappointing odds.

Family disturbances and financial disasters can be extremely disrupting, but very few problems compare to the excruciating experience of the mental disorder. Shadows cast by the troubled mind are always longer than the shadows cast by material losses. Professionals who attempt to heal illnesses of the mind claim that more mysterious agitation is hidden in psychic anxieties than in the impending financial insolvency. The inner world, far more sensitive and complicated than material transactions, has its own motivation. Medical research has discovered many a healing way in the perplexing labyrinth of mental and spiritual trials. Yet a great deal of work is still needed before the physician can lift the heavy darkness that threatens the mind of the afflicted. As long as the more fortunate ones sincerely care for the less fortunate ones, the situation is bound to improve.

Some failures cannot be reversed, and we have to let them be. This does not mean that we should yield to their influence, but a blessed purpose is served if we see these failures as a challenge that can strengthen our determination to conquer the adversity. The very manner in which we allow them "to be" will decide the power of their impact. In a showdown with frustration and serious setbacks, a bold front and a firm decision to cope with the upsetting calamity are pow-

erful assets that help to strengthen the spirit. Deflecting failures from the core of our being to the peripheries of life
renders them less threatening and more pliable to solution.
Such a step takes discipline and freedom of will. People who
harbor a grudge and self-reproach are already ensnared by
the tentacles of misfortune. Unable to put their own house
in order, they become easy prey to the disruptions that circumstances beyond their control inflict upon their lives.

Were we to struggle only on the psychological plateau,
our position would remain insecure and vulnerable. Physical
proficiency and mental acumen offer limited abilities of cop-
ing with the crisis, of letting it be. Providentially, however,
spiritual resources are available that enable us to extract
meaning from tribulation and distress. We who believe in
the Lord are graced to detect a mysterious purpose where
the unbeliever discovers only misfortunes and despair. In
the life of Christ, failures were assigned a redemptive role;
in our lives too, occasional mishaps and disasters carry a
message that helps us to accept and live with the mysteries
of our faith. What seems confusing and useless assumes an
entirely different perspective when considered under the light
of eternity. We can never bring ourselves to love what is
bitter, but the consolation of faith can teach us to view our
failures with understanding and meaning. "And our hope
for you is confident, since we know that sharing our sufferings, you will also share our consolation" (2 Cor. 1:7).

Besides downfalls and defeats, our state of sinning is another dimension of life that we have to let be. Christ stressed
the obvious with His simple statement: "He who denies that
he is a sinner is a liar." We may have denounced Satan, but
Satan never denounced us. Although baptism cleansed us
from the heritage of original sin, it did not restore our *innocence*. The full order and harmony of our mind and will were
not recovered. More often than we like to admit, lingering
weaknesses entice us to seek our own delights even when
such desires are not in accord with our spiritual discern-
ments.

What is the proclivity to sin that always accompanies us

even when it is not invited? Is it a transgression of ancient
traditions inherited from centuries long past? Is it a disregard for the conduct instilled in us by our parents, teachers
and advisors? Is it a contradiction and breach of law that
humanity itself hands on from generation to generation? Indeed, sin is all of these and more: it is a religious offense, a
revolt against moral obligations, a violation that causes guilt
and defiance. God expects us to show our love by keeping
His commandments. He, the fountain of life, the one and
true Creator and Ruler of the universe, has the right to issue
the rules that we, the lowly creatures, are supposed to obey.
"I am Yahweh, your God, you must make no idols" (Lev.
25:55–26:1).

Although we are sinners, we are never helpless prey. In
the lower faculties of our souls, we may remain under the
law of sin and corruption, but in the profound appreciation
of our faith, we cherish the presence of the Holy Spirit. Convinced that we will never be tested beyond our own strength,
we know we can call on a heavenly strength whenever we
are in need of assistance. When Christ sent His Apostles on
their first mission, He warned them not to be afraid of those
who would kill their bodies but were powerless to harm their
souls! "Fear God," He insisted, "who can destroy both soul
and body." If we refuse to call on our merciful Father in
heaven, our preparations to meet the inner conflicts will never
be strengthened. If we invite our Redeemer, the Keeper of
Peace, to link His grace with our battling spirits, we need
not fear the end. A healed past promises a tranquil future.

Converts to Catholicism frequently admit that one of the
hardest things they had to accept was the act of confession.
People born into their Catholic religion may grumble about
the sacrament of penance, but for them it is probably the
one sacrament that they would least want to abolish. Those
who have learned to let life be know from their experience
and studies that only in confession are the feelings of guilt
laid to rest at last. The peace of mind and the joy of heart
that absolution imparts have no substitute. When "guilt feelings" are tranquilized, it only defers the time of their next

appearance; but when the priest, the agent of God, says, "Your sins are forgiven, go and sin no more," genuine harmony of soul is restored. Welcomed back into the circle of friendship with God, the sinner is happy with the knowledge that *guilt*, the heaviest burden of life, is a burden no longer. "Hide your face from my sins, wipe out all my guilt" (Ps. 51:9).

Human nature writes everything many times over. The acts of committing sin and being forgiven are repeated time and again. There is one thing, however, that remains constant in the vast ocean of human weaknesses: the mercy of God. Can we forget how patiently our heavenly Father waited for the return of the prodigal son or how kindly Christ treated Mary Magdalene, the well-known sinner? Remember His question to her, "Where are they who accuse you?" The Pharisee who pretended to be without sin was the only one whom Christ resented.

Our mistakes and failures with their inevitable feelings of guilt prepare a training ground in our hearts for compassion. Our endurance of pain and agony makes us sensitive to the pleas of fellow beings who encounter similar crises. The indifference of heart and the numbness of mind are gradually infiltrated with a greater awareness of the sufferings of others. The fruits grown of tribulation are never private property; they are destined to be shared in common. Once we learn to overcome personal barriers, our example will show others how to master their own conflicts. A willingness to loosen the bonds that cripple our neighbors is a credit in our account with the divine Judge.

It is rewarding to be able to comfort our friends, to assist them in their hour of predicament. The day may arise, however, when our ability to help others is curtailed by our own sufferings and pain. At that moment we will have to prove to ourselves how much we can endure. Whether it is illness or old age that depletes our resources and weakens our courage and vigor, our response must be the same. We have to "let life be," with all its infirmities and distress. After a lifetime of proud independence, it may be humbling for us

to ask for an arm to sustain us, but if an apparent useless-
ness can be accepted as the final purgation, our feebleness
can become a grace.

This part of life will not be easy to live; no one likes to be
a burden. But are we really a burden if we bear patiently
with physical limitations that are beyond our control? It is
not our right to dictate to God how the last years of our lives
should be. It is God's right, as the Creator of life and death,
to write the last lines of the human story. And when we
realize that it is God who burdens others with our needs, all
we can do is let the situation "be" without resistance and
complaint. By responding to those who care for us with
prayers and gratitude for their unselfishness, we may find
that the end of life will initiate a glorious beginning. "Now
that I am old and gray, God, do not desert me; let me live
to tell the rising generation about your strength and power,
about your heavenly righteousness, God" (Ps. 71:18).

On Holy Saturday, the vigil of Easter, impressive cere-
monies of our faith put us in touch with the whole range of
the human experience, all the way from disappointment to
elation. The Church clothed in darkness and silence vibrates
with life as the priest makes a solemn entrance. A hush of
expectancy fills the air as his voice shares in the joy and
excitement of the impending triumph of our Lord: *Lumen
Christi*—light of Christ. With equal happiness, the faithful
respond *Deo gratias*—thanks be to God. The priest continues
up the aisle with candle in hand and proclaims again the
light of Christ and the faithful repeat their thanks to God.
As the priest approaches the steps of the altar, the words
Lumen Christi and *Deo gratias* are intoned for the last time.
With this reassuring melody still ringing in the air, a glitter-
ing burst of light lifts the shroud of darkness and disperses
the gloom of suffering and death. Defeat yields to a new
rising.

This impressive ceremony relives in many respects our own
various experiences in life. First, the threat of anxiety and
fear and then the release; first, the defeats we have to endure and then the triumphs. One seems to lead into the other.

There is only one destiny: *eternity*. We may ignore it, scorn it or repudiate it, but we can never change it. Whether we like it or not, we are marked for immortality. No matter how sins distort our features, God never ceases His efforts to restore in our souls the image of the Divine. Sufferings and joys, celebrations and lamentations serve only one purpose: to make us ready for the life yet to come. At the blessed moments of Calvary, it needed only a few hours to make a saint out of the thief; in the human moments of existence, however, it takes the span of a lifetime for a "child of God" to emerge from our ever-present mistakes, failures and sins. But time is of little consequence as long as we return to Him.

We need you, Lord, today more than ever. Do not give up on us, the so-called Hopeless Generation. Bear patiently with our transgressions until we realize that there is only one light left to illuminate the darkness: *the lumen Christi*, the light of Christ. Be with us in our response of *"Deo gratias."*

Chapter 13

LET GO

Thank God I'm alive
With freedom to grow,
Fulfillment is mine
Since I've learned to let go.

A determination of will and mind to give up something and
let it go is not a spontaneous human reaction that comes
simply by request. The resolve to divest ourselves of attachments is often a hard-fought disciplinary effort that takes
into account the resistance from intense emotions. Not many
of us enjoy being deprived of personal satisfactions. "Letting go" can be a creative ideal to achieve a proper balance
between needs and desires. The individual decision, however, is not really sufficient to curb our physical appetites;
we need the strength of spiritual motivation to overcome our
crafty nature. Religion, considered purely as a traditional
element in the household of our lives, by itself offers little
inspiration in our struggle with the excesses of human passion. Only the deeper encounter with divine power can
prompt us to cope with human follies. The stamina and
courage required to say *no* to ourselves and to others will be
found in our real acceptance of God.

Mental readiness to curtail personal pleasures opens our
inner space to spiritual desires. The joys we give up are not
lost to the future of our fate; they are returned to us as con-
siderable gains. By forcing the ego to forgo a reliance on

people or things, we invite divine power to invade our souls; illusions of self-sufficiency easily yield to the grace of God. By accepting the command "Seek first the kingdom of heaven" as a directive in the search for happiness, we reserve all energy for selflessness and deeper consolations. The freedom thus gained unveils a stability of character and nurtures our yearnings for things that are lasting, not transient.

By God's appointment, we are stewards and not proprietors of things that capture our heart and mind. Our possessions are not owned; they are merely held in control. The soil of the land provides our sustenance, and in return we contribute a share of energy and talent for the good of all. Rights that give us pleasure but disregard the needs of others surely are not sanctioned by God. By overlooking the essential relatedness of all beings, we deny our roots. The other person, friend or stranger, has exactly the same value of humanity as we do, only in another body. What life provides for us, it should also provide for others. If the world community could accept the notion that all of us are only shareholders of the land, poverty would be reduced to a manageable condition. A loving equality will never appear as long as certain groups appropriate more than they need. When the "too-much" remains in the hands of the one, "too little" is left for the hands of the other. Is it any wonder that such inequalities spread animosities and hate?

Christian hope and challenge rest in the just distribution to all of all things available. In mathematical terms, of course, a lasting equality will never be achieved because the diligent and busy worker will end up with more than the less industrious. Equal opportunities, however, are a moral prerequisite regardless of the fact that some people refuse to put them to good use. God's eternal command is violated when even one person is deprived of the chance to improve a personal style of life. Obviously, there will always be people who have more valued possessions because they labor with greater intensity and care. Although hard-earned affluence is compatible with Christian justice, such personal earnings are never exempt from the law of love, a sharing with the underprivi-

leged. Even though Christ warned us that the poor are always with us, we all have a duty to keep their number from
growing.

Avarice never experiences the sense of "enough"; it knows
how to pursue more of everything and sees life as a "do-it-
alone" project. For those who enjoy such inordinate desires,
valuables are hoarded to satisfy cravings, not needs, and a
statute of limitations is never respected. Covetousness dares
not say, "You take it, I have enough," because the mind of
greed cannot realize when it *has* enough. Oblivious of human goodness, the avaricious person puts faith and trust
into bigger and better fortunes. "People who long to be rich
are a prey to temptation; they get trapped into all sorts of
foolish and dangerous ambitions which eventually plunge
them into ruin and destruction" (1 Tim. 6:9).

Occasionally, with the passing of time, avarice is overcome by sadness, and then comes the discovery that fortunes alone never still the hunger of the restless soul. Deeper
and higher aspirations mar the dream of the earthly paradise. The empty soul, cajoled by wealth, remains the singu-
lar proof that life should be more than a stockpiling of profits and dividends. Suddenly, at a moment of great financial
triumph, the wealthy executive who never learned to let go
becomes aware that even though money brings amenities, it
cannot bring *peace*. Only then, as the divine Hunter pierces
the tender web of a frail security with His sharp arrow, is
He perceived as the ultimate meaning of fate and not as a
figment of religious superstition. The message of the Spirit
makes sense when we experience its reality.

The willingness to "let go" does not suggest the idea of
thoughtless living nor does it advocate financial reckless-
ness. Balanced detachment is fully compatible with a comfortable life-style as long as our pleasures are earned by personal diligence and work. Even money put aside for the
liabilities of advanced age is not a contradiction of the spirit
of nonattachment. If love of self is ordinate, it can inspire us
to take reasonable care of our present needs as well as possible indigence. The right Christian discipline will show it-

self in the right use of things. Modest living habits that bring a certain rhythm of security and order contribute to healthy relationships with God, friend and neighbor. The extremes of poverty or riches are what develop and foster personalities lacking in spiritual and mental growth. The totally impoverished person may labor so intensely for survival that thoughts of higher longings cannot be entertained, whereas the person living in luxury rarely feels the need to seek God's divine provisions.

Actually letting go of luxuries or relationships is a preliminary step to a much greater sacrifice. When we yield a share of the things we enjoy for the benefit of others, we exercise our control over conceit and selfishness and encourage the growth of spiritual interests. If nothing changes within us when we relinquish our rights, if our treasures are offered to others simply as an isolated public gesture, we act for effect alone, without enriching the inner character of our souls. Letting go of things is easy when compared to giving up the self.

Our true worth is determined not by the valuables we own but by the quality of our spiritual and moral values. Possessions may sustain our needs, but convictions are governed by integrity and honor. Without the challenge of moral honesty and without the satisfaction of conquering selfishness, we face a lifetime of wasted luxuries and triteness. "Invest your treasure as the Most High orders, and you will find it more profitable than gold" (Eccles. 29:11).

Today, the *yes* is far more popular than the *no;* words of restraint are frowned upon in our many circles of living. The urge to follow a leader is so dictatorial that individualism is rashly disregarded. Not to be accepted by peers dims the vision and frustrates the will to excel. To "be with it" has created such a feverish hunger that the truth which advocates a "giving up" is considered inappropriate. The modern child, ruthlessly victimized by a hedonistic behavior of endorsing everything that pleases the senses, is shielded from the knowledge that accumulated efforts can discipline rampant nature. Why is it so hard for people to learn that the "letting go" of ordinary attractions can give a return far more precious than the joys surrendered? Life, a continuous growing process, is invigorating and refreshing when people are not captivated by its charm. Detachments can result in a turbulent beginning of opportunity, not just an ending of pleasure. Exchanging an existence of plentiful boredom for one of daring and creativity leads to deeper insights and knowledge. Many a glorious happening will be ours if we keep ourselves free for the experience.

"Losing" is not the same as "letting go." Giving up something by choice awakens spirituality; having to give up something because a loss was suffered creates an atmosphere of depression. When people we love or situations of comfort are taken from us, we are left with such anguish and emptiness of heart that the very meaning of life is questioned. Emotions over the death of a loved one, the end of a friendship or the loss of honest earnings threaten our stability so deeply that life seems worthless. Our whole world assumes a different face and we cannot adjust to the new surroundings. The sun has vanished, perhaps never to rise again.

Losses can destroy our life if we allow them the power to break our spirit. Even when bitter in taste and appearance, however, the experience can provide an opportunity for faith to grow and values to deepen. If the grieving process is accepted not as a tragic end but as a necessary preliminary to new discoveries, the sacrifice assumes an entirely new perspective. The very situation bewailed as a loss by human calculation is often considered a valuable fulfillment in the heavenly evaluation. Our belief in the restorative powers of the resurrection can turn many a distressful event into a powerful sign of hope. Doesn't the Word of God remind us that life is not taken away but only changed into life everlasting? Karl Rahner confirms this in his prayer, "Oh God who is to come, grant me the grace to live now, in the hour of your advent, in such a way that I may merit to live in you forever in the blissful hour of eternity."

As strange as it may sound, some people are willing to

give up material goods or opportunities but will refuse to let go of painful memories. When adults of any age dwell in the past and relive real or imagined confrontations, the once minor offenses grow to major proportions. By allowing the shadow of yesterday to cast its darkness on today, they suffer a self-inflicted punishment and a continuation of the rebellion from years long past. By holding onto problems that should have been forgotten, they frustrate the ego with distorted vision and misplaced blame. It takes a mature spirit and compassionate love to let go of tormented recollections and get on with the business of living. God never intended an error in judgment to outlive the deed. As an example of the forgiveness He expects of us, He begged His heavenly Father to forgive those who crucified Him.

Not only do persons or possessions catch our interests, but places also make us happy. A private piece of land, particular locales or memorable landscapes are so fascinating that we forgo promising opportunities in order to remain nearby. The village in which our first love blossomed, the city where we were born or the site of an early success are mementos that keep us alive. Part of our very existence in memory or dreams belongs to the streets we walked when young; how easily our mind returns to where the body is unable to follow. Perhaps more can be learned about a person from love of the homestead and culture than in an open exchange of ideas.

To lose touch with one's past is to lose part of one's heart. The pilgrim uprooted lacks the stability once furnished by the home. Once the chance to go home is lost, there comes the unquenchable hunger of belonging. Is there any hope left to the homeless when all other doors are closed? Such sorrow probably began when Adam and Eve, our first parents, were sent away from their home.

Eventually, almost all of us discover in faith that even a favorite place on earth cannot provide a lasting city. The human tent, the body we are living in, will fold up one day so that we are free to move into our eternal home. The place of many mansions invites us to settle down, to be at home with

Christ. Here on earth we are offered only temporary shelter in preparation for the place where God himself will wipe away the tears. Although the letting go of our earthly habitat is usually considered a loss, it becomes bearable when thoughts of heaven enter our mind!

Transforming the earthly attachment into the heavenly dream does not come easily. How many of us are detached enough to let go of people, places and things we love simply because of possible eternal returns? The immediate joys we love become such an integral part of our personalities that it is difficult to think of giving them up. Isn't a "sure thing" more attractive than a possible future treasure? And yet, the courage to take the risk is inherent in the redeeming message of Christ; time and again He commanded His followers "to give up" in order to gain. But even with the ability to verify His words with miraculous events, this dynamic Orator met resistance and defeat! The Apostles couldn't "give up" completely and neither can we. Is this really so hard to do? Christ the divine Redeemer and Buddha the human sage both expected detachment from things that could soil purity of mind and endanger eternal security. Although there was a difference in their reasons for "letting go," they expected the same results. The Messiah admonished His followers: "Better have little and with it virtue, than great revenues and no right to them" (Prov. 16:8). The Buddhist teacher suggested that his followers should free themselves from desires in order to eliminate sufferings. One wanted to safeguard eternal life and the other offered enlightenment of a better life on earth. The divine wisdom of Christ and the human greatness of Buddha each recognized detachment as one of the most powerful forces of creation. St. Paul, the fearless Roman citizen, confirmed the value of "letting go" when he said "having nothing, I possess everything."

In the historical development of Christian asceticism, two distinct schools have emerged that seemingly are in opposition: those who have already "let go of every possession" and the others who live with possessions without really being possessed. It may be purely academic to set priorities and discover the more productive kind of life-style, but the question will invariably arise: "Which choice makes it easier to achieve the goal of serving God?" A life with few limited necessities may be less disturbing than one that allows general daily comforts. Very possibly, a supreme renunciation that claims "nothing" as its own will support the heroic act of total surrender, whereas the constant exposure to the pleasantries of society will stimulate the hunger for more.

Authentic abandonment of material things is never achieved by natural endeavors alone. Although extraneous personal impulses can increase the desire to let go and encourage divine inspiration to grow and deepen, individual efforts alone are never sufficient. Much more is needed and, if desired, much more will be granted; when we beg for assistance, the spirit of God residing within us provides the courage and the love required to give up our attachments without the feelings of loss. This love, the very purpose of our existence, is the one thing we are expected never to relinquish. To abandon it would negate the whole meaning of creation. As the beginning and end of the inspiration behind our deeds, it enlightens our minds, strengthens our hearts and deepens our resolve to give up the things without which we can live. For the sake of love, shouldn't we be willing to let go of everything else?

Epilogue

Long ago, very long ago, we were told by a heavenly authority that we are not alone in our efforts to cope with the sufferings, failures and successes in our lives. Someone is continuously on our side to guard us, protect us, to lift us up the moment we feel alone and abandoned. Whenever we reach the point of giving up, we hear, "I am your God and you are my people." God himself offers us a covenant in which He is the protector and we are the protected. He assures us of the power in heaven that is concerned about our fate and our most secret wishes and dreams. Whatever happens, regardless of the circumstances that life presents to us, we are never alone. The pleasant and the unpleasant are not blind casualties of good or bad luck; they are divinely assigned functions that work to our favor. Even when our sight is dimmed to the meaning of a human event, divine wisdom and providential foresight draw a purpose and a finality that are often beyond our capacity to grasp.

God's covenant is freely offered; it is never forced upon us. Within the range of our freedom we can accept or decline. God honors our decision until "harvest time" arrives. Only in the end does the divine Judge rule with "powers supreme." If we allow God to move into the center of our being and determine the present and future of our fate, divine grace will make its miraculous powers felt. If we refuse His presence, then God will leave us to ourselves, the worst punishment we can ever experience. Our denial never diminishes the majesty of *God*, it only causes our dignity and valor to suffer. So much is lost that could have been gained.

To be faithful to God's covenant does not necessarily guarantee success in human terms. Surrender to divine love is often accompanied by human tribulations and disappointments. The more we yield to heaven, the less we seem to be rewarded on earth. Those close to God do not always fare the best. Not only the Apostles of old endured persecution and death for their beliefs, the modern apostle also experiences similar human predicaments. Though we were warned that the disciple is not greater than the Master, we ignore the warnings and find ourselves disappointed with divine arrangements. How easily we forget that life, harsh or gentle, always follows God's designs!

There is a lot of depth psychology administered in the venerable halls of human science and yet so little faith. Impressive energies are spent to analyze the hidden crevices of the unconscious, but hardly any attention is paid to the healing powers that rest in a strong belief in God. Physicians seem to forget that anxieties and fears respond not only to medical treatment but also to a trust and hope in God. Faith energies can relieve a troubled human soul just as effectively as the medical tranquilizer. The God within us, the joy beyond limits, not only promises peace but becomes the gift of peace himself. Science has made impressive discoveries and for that we are grateful, but drugs alone will never be in a position to correct all the apprehensions and trials the soul has to endure. The spiritual dimension, so often the root of human conflict, has to be taken into serious account before evaluations can be finalized. Doctor and priest have to work together before the dilemma of suffering and death can be dealt with successfully. Relating to the two worlds, one world alone never suffices to still the hunger of the restless heart.

"A blessing on the man who puts his trust in Yahweh, with Yahweh for his hope" (Jer. 17:7).

Perennially curious human beings will never stop looking for the place where God can be found. Does God live in the glamorous arena of human achievements or does He reside in the ghetto? Does He dwell with the poor or the rich, with the famous or with the infamous? Where is God at home?

Our Redeemer showered His affections most generously on the people who possessed little or nothing. Low earthly ratings evoke high celestial esteem. The outcasts, prostitutes, thieves and the sinners who repented found favor with the Lord that the privileged groups never received. Remember how our Lord left the ninety-nine behind and went after the one who was lost? Why such a strange preference for the people in rags? Are they more open and sensitive to the promise of heavenly riches than are the powerful, surrounded with their glamour? Or have the lonely and abandoned become honest with themselves, with others and with God?

We are so easily impressed by power, honors and possessions. How quickly we bow to those who command influence and massive fortunes. Some people consider those who have little as "little" and judge those who have nothing as "nothing." While Christ saw poverty as an opportunity, others see it as evil. Who wants to be a beggar?

We seldom learn the lessons time can teach. Two thousand years have not taught us enough. The poor remain a majority and they are pitied as ever. The tensions Christ faced, we face. People who have too much are not in a mood to share with people who have too little. The privileged classes want to protect their wealth and the less fortunate are firmly determined to get their share. Manifestos were written and declarations of equality were issued, but how much change has been effected? Francis of Assisi used force against *himself* in order to become detached from the power of possessions; today the revolutionary leaders preach force against *others* to bring about a just balance between prosperity and justice. Greed still hardens the human heart.

Christ knew all too well that laws are totally inadequate to curb the appetites of human selfishness and greed. More is needed, much more, if the rich are to become generous and unselfish; this *more* was first introduced by Christ with the words: *love each other.* This new commandment has to fulfill the almost impossible task of restoring again equality and justice. If the heart does not save us from ultimate destruction, no other power will. When the poor mirror the face of a brother or sister, generosity and sympathy flow freely, but if they are considered unwelcome strangers, harmony is slow to appear. Obviously, legislators and political representatives who appeal for fairness are glaringly ineffective in their efforts to eliminate disturbing inequalities. Love has to be added to any mandate to make such a vehicle successful. People who love one another are not only willing but eager to share. What was said about the early Christians must be heard again from every street on our planet: "Look how these Christians love one another!" Our present predicaments clearly prove that different alternatives are doomed to failure.

What we do and what we say are always a response to God. Our deeds as well as our misdeeds relate to a divine order. We either serve God or we serve an idol. If we sense in the pleading voice of the pauper the commanding voice of God, our generosity will come naturally. When we recognize in the imprints of pain the vestiges of the cross carried by Christ, the Good Samaritan will walk the streets again. Is it fair for anyone to keep for personal delight the things that someone else needs for survival?

Christ never advocated a revolt of the heart to go against the prevailing law. Our Savior always respected the power of constituted authority. What He does demand, however, is the right of the poor to be treated with dignity and assisted with respect. Barriers erected to keep abandoned ones *out* are not only an insult to the forgotten, they are also a serious offense to the preferences of our Lord. What we fail to do for the poor, we fail to do for Christ.

As long as love survives, we will survive. Only hate has

the diabolical capacity to freeze the human soul. Bethlehem is not only a heralded village on the map of Judea; Bethlehem is also that place in time where divine love is born again in our love for others.